ACKNOWLEDGEMENTS

During the preparation for and writing of the report I received much kind assistance from the Commissioners and Staff of the Royal Commission, for which I am grateful. Also, Vito Natrella, the Director of the Statistics Division of the US Internal Revenue Service, kindly arranged for members of his staff to read Chapter 2 of the survey, and their comments proved very valuable. Naturally, I alone am responsible for any remaining errors. Finally, I wish to thank Debbie Sanché who typed successive drafts of this report. Her efficiency and good humour never faltered in the face of the tight deadlines I invariably imposed on her.

CONTENTS

LIST OF TABLES

CHAPTER 1

INTRODUCTION

1   In common with the position in the United Kingdom, knowledge of the distribution of personal wealth in other countries is far less detailed than that which is known about the way personal incomes are distributed. This reflects *inter alia* the fact that the tax system does not, as it does with income, automatically provide a source of information on virtually the complete distribution, and also the lesser attention which has typically been paid in the past to the distribution of wealth. Whatever the reason, however, the implication is that a great deal of caution must be exercised when attempting a comparison of the distributions in different countries such as is offered in this paper. In particular, great care is needed to assess the validity of apparent differences, even where estimates are derived from essentially similar sources.

2   There are three well-known methods of deriving estimates of the distribution. Perhaps the most widely-used is the estate multiplier method which in essence treats the dead as a random sample of the living, the sampling being of course "without replacement". Alternatively, recourse can be made to statistics on investment incomes, from which estimates of the wealth which generated these incomes can be calculated. Finally, there exists the most direct and at the same time arguably the most problematical method, that of sample surveys.[1] In the various countries considered in this paper can be found estimates based on all three methods, and in the USA alone all of the methods have been used in the last fifteen years or so. More frequently however it is the case that estimates from only one method are available. In Canada, for example, we have to rely exclusively on sample survey figures. As a result a comparison between countries of the degree of inequality in the distribution of wealth is a very difficult exercise. Add to this the fact that different countries vary quite considerably in their use of any one method and the reader will appreciate why, in what follows, we prefer not to bring all the estimates together in a "league table" of wealth inequality. Furthermore even where a more restricted comparison is offered, such as that in Chapter 2 for the USA and Canada, extreme caution is urged against reading too much into the outcome.

3   The countries covered in this study are, in alphabetical order: Australia, Belgium, Canada, Denmark, France, Ireland, New Zealand, Sweden, the USA and West Germany. A few further countries do publish estimates of the distribution of wealth, but these were deemed so unreliable as not to warrant inclusion here. For example, in Norway the estimated distribution, based on wealth tax returns, is deficient to the extent that total recorded personal wealth

---

[1]This is not the place for a detailed discussion of the different methods. The Royal Commission on the Distribution of Income and Wealth (hereafter shortened for convenience merely to "Royal Commission") spends a considerable amount of time describing the methods in its *Initial Report* (Royal Commission, 1975).

has recently been less than total taxable income. To the best of our knowledge then, the ten countries listed above, plus the UK, are the only ones for which even vaguely reliable figures are available.

4   Even among these ten countries, however, there exists considerable variation in the quality of the estimates produced. Of these countries, there is little doubt that the USA offers the most reliable figures. For this reason Chapter 2 of our paper concentrates on the USA, comparing and contrasting it with the UK and its North American neighbour, Canada.[2] Chapter 3 concerns itself with the remaining eight countries, although, unlike Chapter 2, no attempt is made to compare the countries with each other or with the UK. In both chapters, as well as reproducing estimates of the distributions in the various countries, we also devote considerable space to the ways in which these countries use the different methods of estimation. This is done in the hope that potential improvements in the estimation of the UK figures may become apparent from the examples of other countries.[3]

5   Chapter 4, the last of the paper, serves as a summary of the main points of Chapters 2 and 3 and also draws some conclusions arising from this summary. As we have said above, no attempt is made to construct an overall comparison of the degree of inequality in the distribution of wealth in the various countries. Such a comparison would lead to many false conclusions which we would not wish to encourage. Instead we present the comparisons we feel we can make, and suggest ways in which the UK estimates of the distribution of wealth might benefit from the adoption of practices used in other countries.

---

[2]This study uses the terms Britain and the United Kingdom interchangeably. (In fact, estate-based estimates for the UK are only available from 1974 onwards.)

[3]One instance of this happening already is the recent decision by the Inland Revenue to change the method of valuation of life policies in the official wealth statistics to one similar to that used in the USA.

CHAPTER 2

THE DISTRIBUTION OF WEALTH IN THE USA AND CANADA

I INTRODUCTION

6   In the USA estimates of the distribution of wealth have been made at different times using all three methods mentioned at the beginning of Chapter 1. In Canada, however, there exist only estimates based on sample survey data. Both countries publish irregular "official" statistics; in the USA these are estate-based and appear as supplemental reports to the statistics on income, while in Canada they are the sample survey estimates referred to above, and are based on data collected in the Survey of Consumer Finances when it is extended to cover assets.

7   The official estimates for the USA have been published for only three years: 1962, 1969 and 1972.[1] They are very limited, covering only the top 5% of the total population,[2] and may for other reasons be somewhat inaccurate. Smith and Franklin for example feel that the multipliers used to prepare the 1962 estimates were too high, resulting in a "significant overstatement of the wealth of persons with over $60,000 gross assets" (1974, p.153). Additionally, the $60,000 exemption limit for estate tax in the USA (the cause of the low proportion of the population covered by the estimates) was raised in 1977 to $120,000 and is due to reach $175,000 by 1981, and this will, unless it is outpaced by inflation, reduce still further the number of people for whom estate tax returns provide any information on wealth.

8   The official estimates for Canada, based on household surveys, exist for 1956, 1959, 1964 and 1970.[3] The scope of the surveys has increased considerably since the first survey was conducted so that temporal comparisons are made particularly difficult. As with all sample surveys it seems, inadequate information and non-response of a non-random nature are significant problems. Podoluk notes for example: "[the] surveys appear to underestimate asset holdings although the estimates are more reliable for widely held assets than for assets with a very skewed distribution" (1974, p. 203). Although there was at one time a federal estate tax in Canada, estate data are no longer available in sufficient detail to allow estimates based on these to be prepared.[4]

---

[1]These estimates are to be found in Internal Revenue Service (1967, 1973, 1976).

[2]In the UK, the estate estimates cover 40–50% of the adult population. On the other hand, the difference in the coverage of total wealth is much less dramatic: around 50% in the USA compared with up to 95% in the UK, if the only exclusion considered is the wealth of those not covered by the statistics.

[3]These estimates are to be found in Statistics Canada (1957, 1960, 1966, 1973).

[4]There are still estate taxes in certain provinces in Canada, and information on estates in Ontario in 1963–4 is contained in Cheng, Grant and Ploeger (n.d.).

9 Reports of unofficial research[5] on the distribution of wealth in the USA have appeared somewhat fitfully, although as we have mentioned already, examples exist of work using all three methods of estimation. The estate data were used by early investigators—Merwin (1939) gives details of these studies—but the first systematic application of the mortality multiplier method, by Mendershausen (1956), came relatively late, at least by comparison with the UK. The method was considerably developed by Lampman (1962), and in particular he introduced the use of national balance sheet data as control totals for the values of different assets. Lampman's estimates, together with those of Smith (1974) provide a series for the shares of at least the wealthiest groups in the population.[6] The investment income method has recently enjoyed a revival of interest with the work of Lebergott (1976) and Wolff (forthcoming). Prior to this it has been relatively little used, except for a period in the 1930s when it was extensively discussed notably by Lehmann (1937) and Stewart (1939). On the other hand there is a strong tradition of survey evidence, dating from the period when the census enumeration included wealth declarations. Soltow notes that the 1860 census, for example, records Abraham Lincoln as having a total wealth of $17,000 (1975, p. 233). The major recent surveys are the Survey of Financial Characteristics of Consumers in 1963–4, the results of which are published in Projector and Weiss (1966), and the Survey of Economic Opportunity conducted in 1967 for the (now defunct) Office of Economic Opportunity.[7]

10 There have been no attempts to estimate the distribution of wealth in Canada other than the official estimates based on the Survey of Consumer Finances, although Davies (forthcoming) makes use of various sources to assess the reliability of the estimates of the distribution taken from these surveys. The absence of any estimates using the estate multiplier method reflects the fact that no suitable estate data are available. It is less easy however to explain the absence of estimates using the investment income method. Size distributions of investment income are available, and information on the asset composition of wealth can be obtained from the household surveys, so that in principle it would be possible to estimate at least the upper tail of the distribution from the investment income data. On the other hand it must be said that the resulting estimates would be potentially subject to large errors because of their dependence on the survey data, the more so if attempts were made to estimate the distributions for years other than those covered by the surveys by interpolating the asset composition from years for which it was available.

11 The remainder of this chapter is organized as follows. In section II we discuss in detail estimates which have been made of total wealth and its distribution in the USA paying particular attention to the data sources and methods of estimation. Then, in section III, we repeat the exercise, this time for Canada.

---

[5]The words "unofficial research" are used solely to distinguish this research from that conducted and published by government agencies and are not to be construed as implying that the work was conducted in a clandestine fashion.

[6]As with the official estimates, coverage is severely restricted by the high exemption level for estate tax, which means that only a small proportion of all deaths are liable for the tax.

[7]Both of these surveys were conducted on behalf of government agencies so that they might more appropriately be regarded as "official" research.

Section IV presents the actual estimates and compares the dispersion with that estimated for the UK; additionally attempts are made to identify the factors which cause the differences which exist between countries.

II ESTIMATION OF THE DISTRIBUTION OF WEALTH IN THE USA

II.1 Studies using the estate multiplier method

The estate tax in the USA

12 Any discussion of estate-based estimates of the distribution of wealth must begin by outlining the implications of the scope and coverage of the estate tax for the wealth covered by the estate data. In the case of the USA the supplemental reports containing the estimates include an appendix on "The Characteristics of Estate Tax Wealth". The most recent report notes that "the estate tax return's use as a data source for the asset holdings of the wealthy is limited because the wealth reported on the return is not identical to what is ordinarily considered one's personal wealth" (Internal Revenue Service, 1976, p. 61). In the following few paragraphs we briefly review the major differences between estate tax wealth and personal wealth in the USA, comparing these with the differences between estate duty wealth and personal wealth in the UK;[8] this comparison is of course important for the assessment of the relative dispersion of estate-based estimates of the distributions in the USA and the UK which comes later, in section IV.

13 The first point to note about estate tax wealth is that, to appear on the estate tax return, the wealth "must have been owned by the decedent at death, and have a value after death" (Internal Revenue Service, 1976, p. 61) except for gifts judged to have been made in contemplation of death. This leads to differences between estate tax wealth and personal wealth in the case of, *inter alia,* joint property, lifetime transfers, pensions and life insurance. We will consider each in turn, but will not yet mention the effect on the estimates of the treatment of these assets by estate tax. This subject will be dealt with when we come to the estimates themselves since in certain cases adjustments are made to bring the definition of wealth more into line with the conventional notion of personal wealth.

14 In those States with community property laws, property is allocated to an individual spouse or to the "marital community" on the basis of whether it was acquired before or during marriage. In the former case the property is retained by the appropriate spouse and becomes liable for estate tax on the death of that spouse, with no special exemption. Property of the marital community, however, is considered to be divided equally between the members of the community so that half is eligible for estate tax on the death of one spouse. Only eight States have community property laws, however, and in the remaining States joint property is (with several exceptions) included at full value in the estate of the

---

[8]Reference is made here to estate duty merely for convenience. The tax has in fact been superceded by the capital transfer tax. However, it is not anticipated that this change will cause serious problems for the UK estimates of the distribution, and capital transfer tax on transfers at death is little different from estate duty.

deceased. The UK treatment of joint propery is different in two respects. First, jointly owned property which passes by survivorship is entirely exempt from estate duty. It must be borne in mind that this is not necessarily all property acquired during marriage since the decision to hold property jointly is a conscious one, taken by the married couple. Thus wealth acquired during marriage can quite easily be the property of an individual spouse and be taxed accordingly. Also this exemption does not necessarily mean that the property is "missed" by the estate duty statistics as, even though probate is not required in the case of jointly-owned property, this will only occur where the "total value together with the free estate does not exceed the level at which duty becomes payable" (Royal Commission, 1975, p. 75).[9] The second way in which estate duty in the UK differs from the estate tax in the USA in its treatment of joint property is that in the UK an extra exemption is allowed if there is a surviving spouse. This allows estates of up to £30,000 (instead of the normal exemption of £15,000) to be free of duty, where at least £15,000 passes to a surviving spouse. Such an estate would very likely be missed by the estate duty statistics whereas, in the USA, the exemption level (currently $60,000) is the same regardless of the relationship of the recipient of the estate to the deceased.

15 The other items mentioned above, lifetime transfers, pensions, and life insurance, are more easily dealt with. In the USA, if a gift is made less than three years before death it is counted as part of the deceased's estate since it is considered to be in anticipation of death. In the UK, however, it was the case that, under estate duty, the gift had to be made more than seven years before death to avoid being included in the estate. Since the introduction of capital transfer tax, all lifetime transfers are taxable, albeit at a lower rate than transfers at death, except that certain exemptions exist, notably those which exclude from tax all transfers between husband and wife and transfers up to a specified limit made by an individual in any one tax year.

16 Pensions and life insurance are assets for which the estate tax valuations are potentially inappropriate in both the USA and the UK, although the extent of the discrepancy depends on whether we are concerned to extend our concept of wealth to assets which the Royal Commission has termed "non-marketable" (1975, pp. 9-10).[10] In both countries most pensions are not counted as part of the estate since, in line with paragraph 13 above, the wealth does not survive the decedent. It follows therefore that no problems of comparability of estimates exist on account of the different treatment of this asset, except to the extent that the holding of wealth in this form is more prevalent in one country than the other *and* we wish to include all or part of it as personal wealth.[11] Life insurance is a slightly more difficult asset. Both the USA estate tax and the UK estate duty value life insurance at the sum assured, but this is only the correct valuation where the holder is deceased and is inappropriate for indicating

---

[9]For most estates, of course, probate is required, so that—unlike the situation in the USA—the UK statistics record many estates which fall below the exemption limit but which nevertheless exceed the limit for probate.

[10]The distinction between marketable and non-marketable assets is related to that between sell-up and going concern valuations used by Atkinson and Harrison (1978a, p. 6).

[11]Clearly a pension is not a marketable asset and hence does not have a sell-up value. Thus the estate tax treatment is the appropriate one if we are counting only marketable assets.

the amount of insurance in the hands of the living. Again therefore the basic treatment in the USA and the UK is the same, but as we note in paragraph 19 below, the official estimates in the USA make an adjustment for life insurance policies to ensure that the valuation is appropriate to the living population. In the UK, only the adjusted series estimated by the Royal Commission and the most recent Inland Revenue estimates are corrected for the over-valuation of life policies.

The official estimates

17   Having discussed the nature of the estate tax in the USA, and in particular its implications for wealth covered by the estate data, we turn now to a consideration of estimates of the distribution of wealth in the USA based on these estate data; we begin by reviewing the official estimates.[12, 13] These are based on a stratified sample of estates filed in 1973, regardless of the year of death of the decedent. The sample comprised over 54,000 returns, about 30% of the total filed. All estates over $300,000 gross estate were selected, while below this level the sampling fraction was 20%. Some returns were excluded after being sampled, for example, where the gross estate was equal to or less than $60,000, suggesting that the return was filed unnecessarily. The practice of using estates filed in 1973 for the estimation of the distribution in 1972 reflects the fact that filing occurs only with some delay.[14] The maximum delay allowable is 15 months from the date of death, although an extension of up to 6 months can be granted. If all filings were made after 15 months then some of those made in 1973 would actually relate to deaths in 1971; if some filings were made after substantially less than 15 months, some would relate to deaths in 1973. However, the Internal Revenue Service argues that past experience supports the assumption that with few exceptions the returns apply to the correct year, and in the case of the 1972 estimates only 6% of the returns applied to deaths in 1971 or earlier years. On the other hand 28% applied to deaths in 1973 (Internal Revenue Service, 1976, p. 1).

18   It must also be noted that even if only 1972 deaths were covered, the date of the valuation may not be 1972. In filing a return an executor can choose to value all assets either (i) at death; or (ii) at 6 months after death,[15] with the added provision that, in the case of (ii), assets disposed of within 6 months are valued at their realisation value. In times of declining asset prices, the choice of (ii) is dictated by the desire of the executor to avoid the tax being calculated on

---

[12]The following review of official estimates is of the most recent (1972) estimates.

[13]We do not propose to discuss the method of estimation in great detail, except to the extent that differences in the method between the USA and the UK affect comparability of the estimates. The estate multiplier method, and its associated deficiencies, are adequately dealt with in the Royal Commission's *Initial Report* (1975, pp. 74–75 and 80–96).

[14]A similar practice is followed in the UK. The estate returns for a tax year, say April 1972 to March 1973, are used for the estimation of the distribution in the calendar year in which the majority of the tax year fell, 1972. Adjustments can be made subsequently and the treatment of them is discussed in Atkinson and Harrison (1978b, p. 14).

[15]In the case of returns used for the 1969 and earlier estimates, this period was 1 year. The change may have been a consequence of the fact that "a larger proportion of estimates used the post-death valuation date in 1969 than in any prior filing year" (Smith. 1974. p.164).

an estate which was worth significantly more when the bequestor died than it currently is to the heir receiving it. Additionally the provision allowing disposition prevents the unnecessary diminution of the estate. Essentially the executor is concerned to minimise the average rate of tax, expressed as a proportion of the realisable value of the estate, which is not necessarily the same thing as minimising the value of the estate, or the actual tax paid. The effect of allowing the executor to choose the date of valuation is undoubtedly to understate the estimate of estate wealth. For example Smith notes that in 1969, "had all estates filed at date of death, gross estate would have been $45 billion higher" (1974, p. 164).[16] However, Smith goes on to argue that this amount is less than one might have expected and attributes this to the fact that realisation for capital gains tax purposes is not deemed to have taken place at death so that the heir only pays the tax if he or she realises the asset. Furthermore the tax is then levied on the gain between the realised value and its value for estate tax purposes so that, if the marginal rate of capital gains tax is higher than the marginal rate of estate tax, it actually pays to *overstate* the size of the estate. This may explain why 486 estates in 1969 chose (ii) rather than (i) "even though it resulted in a higher tax liability" (Smith, 1974, p. 168).

19   Finally, we should mention that, independently of this, an average understatement of values for estate tax purposes is the rule. Estate valuations are unaudited ar.d for 1941 Harriss estimates that auditing reveals an undervaluation of 10% (1949, p. 329). The Internal Revenue Service also calculates that Harriss' technique, in a modified form, yields a figure of 10% for 1962 (Internal Revenue Service, 1967, p. 76). The official estimates are not adjusted for any of these problems of valuation, and hence tend to understate the wealth of top wealth-holders. However, an adjustment is made to deflate the valuation of life insurance policies since, as noted in paragraph 16 above, the estate statistics include the full sum assured, whereas in the hands of the living the policies are worth substantially less. In co-operation with the Institute of Life Insurance, ratios of the cash value to the face value of policies are computed for each of 11 age groups and these are applied to the amounts of life insurance included in the estate statistics. The ratio of course rises with age. For those aged under 30, for example, it is 0.038, rising to 0·263 for those aged 60–64, and for those aged 80 or over to 0·773. In all cases it is computed for the 1972 estimates on the basis of information on policies held in 1971, and the total number of policies used in the analysis is 5,485.

20   The next aspect of the official use of the estate multiplier method to which we must turn our attention is the mortality multipliers. These are the subject of an appendix in the supplemental reports, and the report of the 1972 estimates notes that the population mortality rates have to be adjusted "to correct for the more favourable mortality experience of the wealthy" (Internal Revenue Service, 1976, p. 59), a correction which is also made to most UK estate-based estimates, including the official ones. The derivation of the differentials to be

---

[16]Although Smith uses the term "gross estate", he is actually referring to the gross wealth of top wealth holders since the total gross estate of those covered by the estate tax in 1969 was only $30 billion. I am grateful to the Internal Revenue Service for pointing this out to me.

applied differs between the UK and the USA however. In the former, information from the census on social class mortality is utilised; while in the USA three sets of differentials are used, all derived from information on the mortality of the Metropolitan Life Insurance Company's predominantly male "Whole Life" policy holders (Internal Revenue Service, 1976, p. 59). The three sets are based on different groups of policy holders, specifically: (a) those with $25,000 or more in life insurance (preferred risk), (b) those with $5,000 or more (preferred risk), and (c) those with non-preferred risk life insurance of $5,000 or more. Adjustments to the Metropolitan Life differentials are necessary since they are derived predominantly from information on male mortality and additionally because they refer to the four years from 1969 to 1972 rather than just 1972. The question of which set of differentials to use is decided with reference to certain characteristics of each estate tax return, specifically: age of decedent, size of net worth, and size of insurance.[17] The appendix to the 1972 estimates describes the result as follows: "in very general terms, the effect of this . . . was to give the [group (a) differentials] to individuals who were very wealthy and under age 60 (under age 80 for millionaires); the [group (b) differentials] to individuals who were age 60 and had moderate wealth; and the [group (c) differentials] to those individuals who were age 60 or more and had moderate wealth" (Internal Revenue Service, 1976, p. 60). The proportions of the returns to which the groups of differentials applied were, respectively, less than 5%, almost one-third and almost two-thirds.

21 Finally, mention should be made of the fact that a year's estate tax returns regularly include a small proportion (2% in 1963, 3.7% in 1973) where the age of the decedent at death is not known. For the most recent (1972) estimates, age-unknown estates "were assigned the overall weighted average estate multipliers of the age-known decedents for each sex" (Internal Revenue Service, 1976, p. 60). A similar problem occurs in the UK, although the proportion of estates for which age is not given is rather smaller than in the USA. In the fiscal year 1961-2 for example less than 1% are recorded as "age not stated" in England and Wales although, strangely, the proportion is appreciably higher in Scotland. The practice in the official estimates in the UK is to apply multipliers to this group of estates based on a special investigation of these estates, on the assumption that the results for the particular year of the investigation are also valid for other years.

22 The resulting estimates are of the personal wealth of individuals with gross assets in excess of the exemption limit for the estate tax: in 1972 this was $60,000, and in what follows we will concentrate on a description of the estimates for this year since they are the most recent available.[18] According to the estimates there were 12.8 million individuals in the USA in 1972 with a gross wealth of more than $60,000, representing about 6.1% of the total population. This group had a total net worth of $1,852 billion,[19] and gross assets of $2,152 billion. Of the 12.8 million individuals, 8.0 million had a net worth of less than $100,000,

---

[17]The 1972 official estimates were the first to have been derived using this approach. Earlier estimates were based on only one set of differentials.

[18]Later in the survey, in Section IV, we consider the time-series evidence and contrast this with the evidence for the UK.

[19]Throughout the survey "billion" is used to denote "thousand million".

nearly $\frac{1}{2}$ million had a net worth of $500,000 or over and there were 180,000 millionaires. Other analyses of the results are presented, for example estimates disaggregated by sex and marital status and by types of asset. However, no attempt is made to infer anything about the distribution of wealth among the entire population by using, for example, control totals for national wealth to estimate the percentage of total wealth held by the 12.8 million individuals. Attention is confined to the distribution within this group, termed top wealth-holders, so that for use on a comparative basis the analysis would have to be extended to one of the overall concentration of wealth. Unofficial estimates exist which have made this further step, notably those by Lampman (1962) and Smith (1974) is not an extension of these, since he prefers instead to begin with we can tell, the only official estimates of the share of top wealth-holders as a percentage of the wealth of the entire USA population. Natrella (1975) has calculated these and they qualify as "official" both because of his position (Director of the Statistics Division, Internal Revenue Service) and because they are developed from the official estimates of the wealth of top wealth-holders contained in the supplemental reports. By contrast the unofficial research of Smith (1974) is not an extension of these, since he prefers instead to begin with the basic estate data.[20]

23   Natrella uses national balance sheet information[21] on total net worth of all individuals in the USA to estimate the share of that wealth owned by the group of the population that would have been required to file estate tax returns in 1972—the top wealth-holders. This group of nearly 13 million people constituted 6% of the total population[22] in 1972 and owned over half the total net worth. By comparison the much smaller group of top wealth-holders in 1962 (2% of the total population) owned 40% of total wealth. Within the top wealth-holders Natrella estimates the share of the wealthiest 1% as 30·4% in 1972, compared with 31·4% in 1962 suggesting that concentration of wealth among the very wealthy seems to have remained broadly constant over that 10-year period. There are of course problems associated with this approach, as Natrella is at pains to point out. In particular "it is the nature of [balance sheet] estimates that practically all errors come to rest in the residual segment, individuals" (1975, p. 10). This is equally true in the UK, and Atkinson and Harrison (1978a) have suggested that the Royal Commission is not sufficiently critical of the national balance sheet data it has constructed. However, both the Royal Commission and Atkinson and Harrison use balance sheet data in a more sophisticated fashion than Natrella, who does not allow for the possibility that some part of the difference between the balance sheet figure and the estimated wealth of top wealth-holders should be allocated to these top wealth-holders. A second problem which Natrella cites is that estimates of "holdings of top wealth-holders can be changed considerably by small variations in the estate multipliers" (1975, p. 10). This is indeed true but it is equally the case that the estimates of the *numbers* of top wealth-holders will also be changing. The net

---

[20]Lampman's (1962) work is not relevant here since the official estimates were first prepared for 1962 whereas Lampman's estimates extend only to 1956.

[21]This data is discussed in more detail later, in section II.4.

[22]Estimates of the shares of the wealthiest groups in the UK are usually in terms of the adult population so that the USA figures need a simple adjustment to make them comparable.

result on percentage shares is often small (although not negligible). Atkinson and Harrison for example conduct a fairly exhaustive theoretical and empirical study of mortality multipliers and conclude that changes in multipliers "do not—despite the substantial changes in the estimates of total wealth—lead to widely differing estimates of the share of top wealth-holders" (1978a, p. 77). It may be therefore that Natrella's figures are more robust than he gives them credit for.

Unofficial estimates

24　We turn now to the more developed side of the use of the estate multiplier method in the USA, the unofficial estate-based estimates. The earliest attempt to make use of estate statistics was that of Spahr (1896) which is described at length in Merwin (1939). Spahr used data on probated estates in New York State to infer a distribution of wealth in the USA. Merwin describes his work as "statistically more pretentious" than earlier research by Holmes (1893) based on census data, but continues that "in transformation . . . into one for the entire country, the statistical manipulations are hard to perceive" (1939, pp. 8–9). Other estimates followed, also utilising estate data but it appears that for the most part researchers were unaware that "the distribution of wealth among decedents was far from being the distribution of wealth among the living" (Merwin, 1939, p. 12), at least until King's work on the distribution in the 1920s was published (King, 1927). Even so, by the start of the Second World War, a full use of the estate multiplier technique for the USA was still awaited. This came with the work of Mendershausen (1956). As Lampman notes: "earlier investigators had used estate tax data, [but] none of them had used [the estate multiplier] method" (1962, p. 10). We do not intend to discuss Mendershausen's work in detail however since Lampman's estimates improved upon it, notably as a consequence of a separate development, "the completion of a set of national balance sheet accounts for a limited number of benchmark years" (Lampman, 1962, p. 10). Lampman was therefore able to pioneer the use of this data, disaggregated by asset type, as an indication of the wealth missed by the estate tax statistics. This lead has of course been followed by, *inter alia,* Smith (1974) for the USA, and the Royal Commission (1975) and Atkinson and Harrison (1978a) for the UK.

25　Lampman's research is based on estate tax returns, the nature of which has already been discussed, so that we will confine ourselves here to differences between Lampman's use of the estate multiplier method and that of the Internal Revenue Service in the official estimates. The first, and probably the major, difference is that the adjustments to the basic "all-whites" mortality multipliers which Lampman makes are based on the mortality of upper occupational groups as well as on that of the holders of large insurance policies. In line with the findings of Revell (1967) for the UK, the latter are lower than the former, implying higher multipliers when insurance data alone are used. Lampman in fact uses mortality rates midway between those for the two groups as his "adjusted mortality rates"[23] with the result that his multipliers are somewhat lower than those based solely on insurance data (such as those used in the official

---

[23]The precise details are given by Lampman (1962, p. 46–7). He also presents separate estimates of, for example, the total number of top wealth-holders and their wealth based on the "all-whites" mortality rates.

11

estimates had they been calculated for the years Lampman studies).[24] From his remarks in a comparison he makes with British estimates based on unadjusted multipliers Lampman clearly thinks that the use of the adjusted rates necessarily increases the estimated concentration (1962, p. 212n). This is not the case, however, and indeed experiments with various sets of multipliers by Atkinson and Harrison (1978a, ch. 3) generate the reverse result.

26   As in the official estimates, Lampman uses a multiplier for the estates for which age is not given, based on the assumption that "the age distribution within the age-unknown group is the same as among those for whom age was specified" (1962, p. 55). Another adjustment which he discusses in terms of multipliers and which is also made in the official estimates is that to reduce life insurance policies to their equity values. Lampman follows Mendershausen by utilising a study made in 1944 of one particular insurance company's ordinary policies, disaggregated by age group. However "after consideration of the several issues involved" (1962, p. 55), Lampman revises downwards the ratios implied by this study, mainly because of the fall in the reserve ratio for all life insurance between 1944 and 1956.[25] Next Lampman makes a number of further adjustments which, like that for the value of insurance policies, are intended to approximate more closely wealth in the hands of the living. Most of the adjustments are not ones made in the official estimates, and it is of further interest to note that Lampman divides the adjustments into ones which convert basic wealth (i.e. unadjusted estate tax wealth) into prime wealth, and ones which convert prime wealth into total wealth. The distinction between prime and total wealth is in fact close to that mentioned earlier between marketable and non-marketable assets: prime wealth is that "owned outright and over which the owner has full power of disposal" while total wealth also includes "wealth to which a person does not necessarily have actual title but in which he has an income interest" (1962, p. 57).

27   Of these adjustments the only one which is also made by the Internal Revenue Service when compiling the official estimates is the exclusion of estates with less than $60,000 gross estate. Among the others made by Lampman are:

(i) the exclusion of estates which have fallen below $60,000 because of the life insurance adjustment;

(ii) an addition of 10% to estate tax wealth to compensate for under-reporting, in line with Harriss' estimate discussed in paragraph 19 above.

---

[24]The problems of using the mortality of upper occupational groups to adjust the multipliers are discussed in Internal Revenue Service (1973, p. 72). In particular, reference is made to inconsistencies caused by: (i) differences between the occupation reported at the Census and that given on the death certificate; (ii) the treatment of retired persons; and (iii) occupational mobility.

[25]The main estimates Lampman presents are actually for 1953, but a time series covering various years between 1922 and 1956 is also calculated.

Also the addition of extra individuals to the top wealth-holders group plus their wealth (as a result of the 10% revaluation lifting them over the exemption level), based on an extrapolation of the frequency distribution and an estimate by Harriss that half of all estates require no auditing change;

(iii) an addition to take account of gifts made in contemplation of death but not deemed to be so by the estate tax;

(iv) a deduction of wealth in the form of personal trust funds, annuities, and pension funds included in estate tax wealth "to 'purify' the prime wealth estimate" (Lampman, 1962, p. 75); and

(v) an addition of the full amount of the items in (iv) allocable to those with estate size in excess of $60,000 to give an estimate of total wealth.

The overall effect of these adjustments is to raise the estimated number of persons by 10% and estimated wealth by 30%.

28   In many ways Lampman's estimates are more sophisticated than those of the Internal Revenue Service although, as he himself notes: "several of the adjustments are necessarily crude and some turn upon quite arbitrary assumptions" (1962, p. 63). More recently Smith (1974) has produced detailed estimates for 1969 which are based on techniques similar to those used by Lampman. For example, the adjusted mortality rates Smith uses are midway between those for "high status occupations" and those for "affluent individuals" buying life insurance policies from the Metropolitan Life Insurance Company (Smith, 1974, p. 157). As we have already noted (in paragraph 25 above), higher multipliers are implied when insurance data alone are used, so that Smith's multipliers are lower than those based solely on life insurance data, such as are used in the official estimates. This is the basis for Smith's suggestion in a joint paper with Franklin that the Internal Revenue Service multipliers for 1962 and 1969 are too high (Smith and Franklin, 1974, p. 163n), although again, as with Natrella (1975), there seems some misunderstanding about what excessively high multipliers imply for percentage shares of wealth and the Lorenz curve. An additional adjustment Smith makes to the multipliers is to take "explicit account of marital status differentials" (Smith, 1974, p. 158) since this factor was found to be extremely important. For instance in the age-group 25–34, the married women mortality rate was 87% of that for all women in that group while for single women the rate was 179% of the overall mortality.[26] As Smith notes, however, with the exception of this marital status adjustment, his multipliers are broadly equivalent to Lampman's.[27]

29   Some of Smith's other adjustments have been discussed already, in connection with the official estimates and/or Lampman's estimates. Life insurance policies are reduced to equity values on the basis of information supplied to the Institute of Life Insurance by a number of large insurance companies; Harriss'

---

[26]These figures relate to 1959–61 and are taken from Klebba (1970). Smith assumes the same differentials apply in 1969.

[27]In the UK only the most recent Inland Revenue estimates incorporate the use of multipliers adjusted for marital status.

(1949) estimate of 10% under-reporting is used to adjust returns upwards. One significant modification to the procedure used in other estimates however is introduced to deal with the question of whether the year of death is the year for which estimates are being made, a point discussed above in paragraph 17. Smith notes that the estate data he uses for his 1969 estimates in fact contain returns for people dying up to 15 years previously, and tests his belief that length of delay in filing returns is positively correlated with size of estate. He finds that the mean estate for 1968 deaths was significantly above that for deaths in 1969 but that for deaths in earlier years the reverse is true, even when the estates are valued in constant 1969 dollars. The problem is therefore "less serious than once thought" (1974, p. 70) but nevertheless is sufficiently important to require some adjustment. In consequence Smith converts all estates relating to deaths in years other than 1969 to their 1969 value with the use of a variety of price indices. The results of all these adjustments are the estimates of the wealth of the so-called "super-rich" [28] in 1969. Smith then takes the asset estimates and compares these with national balance sheet figures for all persons to determine the percentage share of wealth held by this group. For purposes of comparison Smith also presents estimates of the wealth of top wealth-holders. The difference between the two groups is significant. The super-rich numbered 5 million in 1969, and owned net worth totalling over $1,000 billion[29]; the corresponding figures for top wealth-holders are 7 million and over $1,060 billion. The amount of net worth estimated in the hands of the super-rich represented 32.6% of total net worth, and the super-rich constituted 4% of the adult population,[30] or 2.5% of the total population.

30   Finally in this discussion of estate-based estimates for the USA, mention should be made of estimates published elsewhere by Smith, in collaboration with Franklin, of the concentration of personal wealth for various years between 1922 and 1969 (Smith and Franklin, 1974). For years before 1953 the figures are taken directly from Lampman's time series of the shares of top wealth-holders; for 1953 and 1958 the more detailed estimates of, respectively, Lampman, and Smith (1966) are used; while for 1962, 1965 and 1969 new estimates are made. In the case of 1969 the figures differ from the finally adjusted estimates in Smith (1974) since the concern is with changes over time, so that they sacrifice "best estimates for individual years to achieve consistency over the time series" (Smith and Franklin, 1974, p. 162n). The authors note that there is a downward bias from "best" estimates of 10–15%, with the result that they present "a time series. . . which understates the degree of concentration in any given year but is consistent and permits comparisons over time" (1974, p. 163). In our discussion of the estate-based estimates of the distribution of wealth in

---

[28]This group is distinguished from "top wealth-holders" in that members of the former group have *net* worth over $60,000. Lampman considered the broader group which additionally includes those with net worth below $60,000 but *gross* assets over $60,000. The official estimates also cover all top wealth-holders.

[29]This, and other figures for net worth are estimated without making two of the adjustments mentioned above. The effect of these, to take account of date of death and under-reporting, is to raise the $1,000 billion to nearly $1,150 billion.

[30]All persons aged 20 and over on July 1, 1969.

the USA, and how they compare with those for the UK, in Section IV we will use the series presented by Smith and Franklin, [31] plus the more detailed figures for 1969 given in Smith.

II.2 Sample surveys

31 As we noted in the introduction, evidence on the distribution of wealth in the USA from surveys has a long history dating back to the 19th century when census enumeration included wealth declarations. More recently Surveys of Consumer Finances have sometimes covered asset holdings, and the 1953 results were used by Lampman (1962) in a comparison with his estate-based estimates. Evidence from the same year's survey was also compared with that derived by the Oxford Savings Survey for 1954 by Lydall and Lansing (1959). In consequence, at least for 1953, it is possible to make comparisons between the USA and the UK on the basis of both evidence from the use of the estate multiplier method and that from sample surveys, and in Section IV we briefly survey the findings of Lampman, and Lydall and Lansing. In this section, however, which is concerned primarily with the methods rather than results, we confine ourselves to the two most recent surveys, the 1963–4 Survey of Financial Characteristics of Consumers (SFCC) and the 1967 Survey of Economic Opportunity (SEO).[32] Both are very comprehensive sources of direct information on wealth in the hands of the living, and the SFCC has been described by one economist as "the single best source of data on the distribution of private wealth in the United States" (Taussig, 1976, p. 5).[33] However the same writer later remarks that the SFCC is still "far from an ideal source of wealth inequality" (1976, p. 7) since it suffers (as does the SEO to an even greater extent) from many of the usual problems encountered by sample surveys, notably under-reporting of a non-random nature. On the other hand it is probably fair to say that, given the limited coverage of the estate-based estimates, the sample survey figures on the distribution of wealth in the USA are an important independent source in the USA, rather than a "valuable supplement" (Royal Commission, 1975, p. 78) as they are in the UK.[34]

32 The results of the SFCC are published in Projector and Weiss (1966) and report estimates of the "size and composition of wealth of the civilian non-institutional population . . . on December 31, 1962" (1966, p. 1). These are based on a sample of 2,557 consumer units, where consumer unit is defined as groups "of two or more persons related by blood, marriage, or adoption, and residing together" plus individuals "not living with relatives" (1966, p. 2). The survey was notable in that a deliberate attempt was made to sample those groups in the population expected to have large wealth-holdings at much higher

---

[31]Additionally Smith has extended the time series to 1972 and the preliminary estimate for this year is cited in Taussig (1976).

[32]We have learned from correspondence with Professor Sheldon Danziger that a new survey, the Survey of Income and Education, also contains information on wealth and will be released in the near future.

[33]Our discussion of sample surveys in the USA is largely based on Taussig's paper.

[34]This is true both because the UK estate estimates are more comprehensive and hence more trustworthy, and because the sample survey estimates in the UK (the most recent of which relate to the early 1950's) are probably less reliable than those obtained in the USA.

15

rates than for the population generally. Without such differential sampling rates the 2,557 units would have included only about 50 with wealth in excess of $100,000, whereas completed interviews were conducted with 532 such units. The basic data, appropriately weighted, yield estimates of wealth for both the total population and groups within that population, and the main tabulated information presents this for consumer units classified by income, age and employment status of the head of the family.

33   The definition of wealth used in the SFCC is described by Projector and Weiss as "the broadest that seemed possible within the limits of the knowledge people have or are willing to obtain about their holdings" (1966, p. 2). The assets and debts are grouped into six major groups: (a) homes; (b) automobiles; (c) businesses or professions; (d) liquid assets ('current' and savings accounts and US savings bonds); (e) investment assets (marketable securities, investment real estate, and mortgages); and (f) miscellaneous assets (mainly personal trusts). The valuation used is for the most part a market one; one asset which provides problems in this respect however is 'businesses and professions' and here book values are finally used since so few people were able to provide "any meaningful estimate of the price for which their business might be sold" (1966, p. 45). Three other aspects of how wealth is measured in the SFCC must also be briefly mentioned. First, the information obtained on the value of holdings of life insurance, annuities and pensions was so unsatisfactory that it is omitted from the wealth totals. Projector and Weiss therefore present this separately, noting that reviews of the data on these assets reinforce their feeling that they are less reliable than for other assets. Secondly, the classification given above ignores a number of items which are obviously ones that should have been included in the survey had not the "burden of supplying value estimates" been so great. Projector and Weiss draw particular attention to household equipment, furniture, clothing, boats, sports equipment, jewellery, works of art, coins and stamps. Thirdly, wealth in the survey is assets net of debts secured by those assets.[35] Thus, as Taussig points out, "survey wealth is *not* identical to net worth in that other debts are not deducted from wealth-holdings" (1976, p. 6). However, the unsecured debts are considered in some tabulations, and Projector and Weiss reassure readers that "conclusions drawn from distributions by net worth and by wealth are generally the same" (1966, p. 3).

34   In general therefore the coverage of wealth in the SFCC seems poorer than that obtained from estate tax returns although against this it must be said that the Survey does an immeasurably better job of covering the population than do the estate-based estimates. One further shortcoming of the SFCC (and all other surveys) severely reduces the reliability of the information it offers however. In the words of Projector and Weiss "comparison of aggregates based on this survey with those from institutional sources . . . indicates that the under-reporting of liquid assets and instalment debt that has characterised other financial surveys is also a problem in this Survey" (1966, p. 2) although they suggest that response bias, potentially the more serious problem, was minimised by the sample design, by the use of detailed questions on assets

---

[35]Three-quarters of these debts were mortgages on owner-occupied housing.

likely to be held by the wealthy, and by the valuation method. However, this optimism seems not to be shared by Ferber *et al.* who made studies of the accuracy of reported holdings, as a sequel to the SFCC,[36] for savings accounts (1969a) and share holdings (1969b). In effect they began with data on known holdings by consumer units, and then interviewed the holders to see what they reported. Although the results need to be qualified in certain respects, they indicate that, in the case of share holdings, "substantial response and non-response errors exist in the reporting of . . . ownership, . . . the principal sources of these errors are non-reporting by respondents and *the much larger holdings of non-respondents than of respondents,* and that methods are needed to supplement the usual survey methods to correct for this bias" (1969b, p. 431, our stress). A virtually identical conclusion is drawn from the study of savings accounts (1969a, p. 444). The error in the average holdings as estimated from the respondents is an understatement of 46% for the mean balance in savings accounts, and 35% for the average number of shares. The breakdown of the error between sources, given in Table 1, is similar for the two types of assets. Over half the errors are the consequence of the non-reporting of holdings and the rest arise mainly because the holdings of non-respondents on average exceed those of respondents. From their studies Ferber *et al.* also note that size distributions for individual assets are badly biased, in the main because of non-reporting, which interestingly tends to be highest in the tails of the distribution in the case of share holdings. They clearly feel that better survey techniques alone will not eradicate these sources of error since they conclude: "improvement of survey procedure can only go so far . . . The answer would seem to lie in the development of more powerful analytical models for detecting and correcting errors" (1969b, p. 432).

35 The second major survey in the 1960s which yielded information on the distribution of wealth was the 1967 Survey of Economic Opportunity (SEO). This was conducted for the Office of Economic Opportunity by the Census Bureau, and sampled about 30,000 households, of which 18,000 were a 50% random sample of the February and March, 1967, Census Current Population Surveys. These 18,000 households "can be identified and used directly to obtain estimates of national aggregates for the civilian non-institutional population in 1967 for all characteristics of that population covered by the Survey" (Taussig, 1976, p. 9)[37]. Although some 19th century censuses contained questions on net worth, the SEO was the first census survey in the USA this century to include such questions. In many ways the SEO was superior to the SFCC: its sample size was much larger and the amount of information it requested from respondents was much more comprehensive. Additionally the two surveys are largely comparable in terms of the definitions of the consumer unit and wealth. Unfortunately, in one important respect, the SEO falls down badly by comparison with the SFCC, and this is "the quality of the wealth data actually

---

[36]To be quite precise, the work by Ferber *et al.* is to be seen as a check on the "reliability of the data collection techniques" of the SFCC (1969b, p. 416) rather than as a check of the data themselves.

[37]For our discussion of the SEO we are forced to rely on the description given by Taussig (1976) since we were unable to locate any source publications concerned with the scope and methods of the survey.

17

TABLE 1

ALLOCATION OF ERROR BY RESPONSE GROUP

	Percentage of error in estimated mean	
	Number of shares	Mean balance in savings accounts
Errors in average holdings reported ..	−0·2%	−1·7%
Errors in estimation of holding where existence but not amount reported	1·0%	1·9%
Non-reporting of holdings	61·2%	59·7%
Non-respondents:		
Refusals	21·7%	29·8%
Other	16·3%	10·3%
Total	100·0%	100·0%

Source: adapted from Ferber *et al.* (1969a, Table 4, and 1969b, Table 7).

elicited from respondents" (Taussig, 1976, p. 11). Non-response was experienced in about 25% of the sample for questions relating to wealth, and checks indicate that the non-response was not random, being particularly severe in high income and wealth families. In consequence, even more so than in the SFCC, we must treat analyses of the distribution of wealth based on the SEO[38] with a considerable degree of scepticism. Our conclusion therefore is that, even in the USA where estate-based estimates are much less comprehensive than in the UK, data on estates remains the primary source of information on the distribution of wealth when we are interested in the upper tail of the distribution. As a result, the comparison between the USA and the UK we present in Section IV is of estimates derived from the estate multiplier method.

II.3 The investment income method

36 With the exception of the work of Lebergott (1976) and Wolff (forthcoming) this method of estimating the distribution of wealth has recently tended to be ignored in the USA, in direct contrast to the pre-Second World War period when it was adopted by, *inter alia,* Lehmann (1937) and Stewart (1939). The latter in fact suggests that, although it is "inherently less desirable" than estate multiplier or sample survey techniques, the investment income method "has proved the most useful method in working with the existing American materials" (1939, p. 102). Since the method has been little used in recent years, we will consider it only briefly, before passing on to a similarly brief discussion of miscellaneous sources in Section II.4.

[38]See, for example, Terrell (1971).

37 Before Lehmann's work, a number of complicated attempts had been made to estimate the distribution of wealth by capitalising income. Stewart (1939) suggests that this approach was followed, rather than the estate multiplier method because the necessary material for the latter (i.e. information on the mortality of the wealthy) was not available, and because of the limited coverage of the USA estate tax. Even at that time, Stewart acknowledges, "this limitation [was] not present in the English estimates" (1939, p. 101). Lehmann considerably simplifies the general approach to construct an estimate for the USA in 1930 as a "short-cut . . . combining the results of the federal income tax statistics with the results of the federal estate tax returns" (1937, p. 161). He proceeds by first applying a yield multiplier (the reciprocal of the yield) to dividend income shown on income tax returns which gives the capitalised value of corporate stock. Then, from estate tax returns, he calculates the proportion of net estate held in the form of corporate stock, and with this information converts the values of corporate stock into values of net estate for each income class. Stewart (1939) adopts a slightly more sophisticated, but essentially similar, procedure. He plots on a double logarithmic scale the average corporate stock in each estate class against the corresponding net estate; calculates the average corporate stock by income class from a capitalisation of the dividend income; derives the average estate for each capitalised average corporate stock as an estimate of average wealth of the persons in the appropriate income bracket; multiplies the average wealth by the number of persons in each income class to give the total wealth in that class; cumulates the number of persons and the total wealth, and plots the results, again on double logarithm paper. This last exercise then allows of "a limited measure of extrapolation if it is desired to compare the same number of income recipients over several years" (1939, p. 109).

38 Stewart considers a number of difficulties associated with the approach but seems relatively unconcerned about what is perhaps the major shortcoming: the use of the asset composition of estates as an indication of the asset composition of wealth. Stewart remarks that "the critical assumption is merely that in the estates of the living and dying, corporate stock represents about the same proportion of the net estate for each income-wealth class" (1939, p. 108). However, Revell (1962) has shown that the systematic variation of portfolios with age leads to a serious distortion when estate data rather than wealth data are used, with the asset proportions of the elderly receiving too much weight. In particular Revell demonstrates that, in the UK at least, assets such as unquoted company securities are understated. It is for this reason that Atkinson and Harrison (1978a, ch. 7), when making recent estimates for the UK using the investment income method, rely instead on information on the asset composition of wealth derived from applying the estate multiplier method to the estate data disaggregated by asset type.

39 As we have said, other difficulties exist to which Stewart pays more attention. For example, the estate data are deficient as an indication of the proportion of wealth held as corporate stock in the upper and lower tails of the distribution of estates. At the upper end, the curve that relates average corporate stock and average net estates does not extend far enough to accommodate some of the highest values of capitalised corporate stock, so that extrapolation of the curve is necessary. At the lower end, a similar problem occurs because of the high estate tax exemption (at that time, $50,000). This latter problem is perhaps more

19

serious, and Stewart suggests that "it is in this connection that the method requires supplementation by other methods" (1939, p. 111). A further difficulty with the investment income method is the estimation of the rate of yield of corporate stock, and indeed Stewart sees this as the major possible source of error in his estimates. Overall, these and other problems inevitably cast serious doubts on any use of the investment income method, but it is nevertheless valuable since it provides a largely independent check on the estate multiplier method.

40   Finally, in our discussion of the investment income method, we should briefly mention the recent use of the method by Lebergott (1976, pp. 215–247).[39] He takes estimates of total household wealth held in a variety of assets for 1970, and allocates these aggregates across different income groups in the distribution of income based on personal income tax returns, but slightly modified according to Census distributions of family units by income size to take account of the missing families in the lowest income groups who are exempt from filing returns. The allocation method varies with the type of asset. That for corporate stock, for example, is based on the distribution of dividends and "other distributions reported on 1970 individual income tax returns" (1976, p. 226) while business equity is allocated by income level using tax data for net profit of businesses, professions, farms and partnerships. The allocations are often quite arbitrary, and are frequently heavily qualified by Lebergott. The outcome however is of considerable interest, although it suffers from his decision to give his results as wealth-holdings at different income levels. If instead a distribution of wealth in terms of wealth levels were derived it would be of greater use, since it would allow a comparison with results from the estate multiplier method.

II.4   Miscellaneous sources

41   In addition to those studies already cited, there exist a number of miscellaneous sources on various aspects of the distribution of wealth. Additionally we must make some mention of national balance sheet data, which, although they are not directly concerned with the distribution of wealth, are nevertheless widely used in the construction of estimates of the distribution, particularly when the major source is one which only covers part of the wealth-holding population. This is, of course, the use to which the data are put when estimates are made from the estate multiplier method, an approach pioneered by Lampman (1962). Also, however, they can be utilised as wealth aggregates to be distributed on the basis of independent information as Lebergott (1976) does.

42   The first major attempt to compile a comprehensive balance sheet for the USA was that of Goldsmith (1956), who has continued in the forefront in subsequent developments of these data. This first study contains estimates for six "benchmark" years between 1900 and 1949, and these are the figures used by Lampman, together with preliminary estimates from an early stage of a new project by Goldsmith. Then, in the early 1960s, a series of reports began to appear containing details of this research by Goldsmith (and others) into post-

---

[39]Work by Wolff (forthcoming) unfortunately came to our attention too late to be included in the survey.

war capital market developments in the USA. Of particular interest here is Goldsmith and Lipsey (1963) which presents annual balance sheets for 1945 to 1958, and in so doing updates the postwar estimates in Goldsmith (1956). The basic form of the balance sheets in Goldsmith and Lipsey has been followed ever since, for example in Federal Reserve Board (1972), the data used by Lebergott. One particular problem associated with the household sector, as defined by Goldsmith, is that it includes foundations and non-profit organisations, and, although this is often ignored by users of the data, Smith (1974) "extracts" an individual sector from the household sector, and notes that work is in progress at the Federal Reserve System to do this in a more detailed way. Since the national balance sheet data are not the major concern of this particular study, we do not propose to discuss them any further. An extensive discussion of the basic problems in their compilation, covering such matters as sources, methods of valuation, and reliability, is to be found in Goldsmith and Lipsey (1963, pp. 13–40).

43   There exist a number of other sources of information on certain aspects of the distribution of wealth in the USA, of which three are of sufficient interest to cite briefly here. The first of these is a report on a survey, conducted in 1964 for the Brookings Institution, of the affluent, or more precisely individuals with incomes of $10,000 or higher in 1961 (Barlow, Brazer and Morgan, 1966). The sampling was roughly proportional to income to ensure a disproportionately large number of interviews with individuals with very large incomes. Questions were asked on the composition of portfolios, but, except in the case of common stock, fixed-yield assets and real estate, the sizes of the holdings are unknown. Even for the assets listed, the respondent was only asked to say whether the holdings were under $10,000, $10,000 to $100,000, or over $100,000, so that direct knowledge of the distribution of wealth is little advanced. What is of interest here however is that those interviewed were also asked to say what the primary source of their wealth was—gifts and inheritance, savings, or capital gains. Only 7% mentioned gifts and inheritance alone, and extra questioning suggested that around one-seventh of the aggregate wealth of the entire group came from this source, although those individuals with very large wealth ($500,000 or more in common stock alone) attributed much greater importance to gifts and inheritances, and particularly the latter. Of these, 28% said that one-half or more of their wealth was derived from gifts and inheritances. To anticipate our discussion of influences on the distribution of wealth in Section IV therefore it seems that, except at the very top of the distribution, inheritance is relatively unimportant.[40]

44   The remaining two studies are, by comparison with research previously cited, far more imprecise. Lundberg's (1968) mammoth study of the rich, is concerned with such matters as the methods by which the likes of Paul Getty

---

[40]Similar conclusions are contained in the results of the SFCC (Projector and Weiss, 1966, p. 148), although both these results and those of Barlow, Brazer and Morgan, because they are based on survey data, probably understate the true importance of inheritance. Davies (1978) considers this problem and suggests that the level of inherited wealth may be $2\frac{1}{2}$–$3\frac{1}{2}$ times the survey figures (see below, paragraph 69).

and Haroldson Hunt acquired their massive wealth-holdings, the relationship between crime and wealth, and the importance of inheritance for Lundberg's "super-rich",[41] as well as many other aspects. Similarly Louis (1968) reports interviews with 153 centi-millionaires, but, although there are many interesting observations on the methods of wealth accumulation by the very rich, there is clearly no basis for presuming that the results are more generally applicable.

III ESTIMATION OF THE DISTRIBUTION OF WEALTH IN CANADA

45 As we have mentioned earlier, the only data available in Canada on the distribution of wealth are those collected through household surveys on the occasions that these surveys have been extended to cover wealth. Only limited data ever existed on estates, and the federal government has "vacated the field of estate duties" (Podoluk, 1974, p. 203), so that the sample surveys, conducted in 1956, 1959, 1964 and 1970, assume an importance far in excess of that of equivalent surveys in countries with well-developed estate data, such as the UK. Of the four surveys, the first three were restricted to the non-farm population; the most recent one however was representative of the total population. Other differences between the surveys render comparison over time difficult, particularly the fact that the types of assets covered have expanded primarily liquid assets in 1956 to "a very comprehensive list of wealth components" by 1970 (Podoluk, 1974, p. 204). The general problems of sample surveys are no less severe in the Canadian case, so that Podoluk, in her discussion of the results from the surveys, is forced to offer the justification for their continued existence that "imperfect as [they] are, they are the only existing Canadian sources of data on the distribution of wealth" (1974, p. 210). While this statement seems perhaps unnecessarily apologetic, it does convey an impression of uncertainty about the results which appears justified in the light of the work of Davies (forthcoming), discussed below in paragraph 49.

46 In this report we will confine ourselves to a discussion of the 1970 survey, the results of which are published in Statistics Canada (1973).[42] The sample consisted of 12,626 occupied households, of which 2,664 were not interviewed for various reasons, including a complete refusal to respond, or were interviewed, but provided incomplete income information. The remaining 9,962 were those which supplied complete income information, a response rate of 74·9%, but as is usually found, the response rate for assets was lower. Of the 23,576 individuals aged 14 or over in the 9,962 households, 67·8% (30·8%) provided full details of assets (debts), 28·7% (68·8%) had no assets (debts), and 3·7% (0·7%) refused to answer some or all of the asset (debt) questions. Where refusal was encountered, missing asset and debt data were assigned to a non-respondent from the record of a respondent considered to be similar. The criteria used to locate a similar individual included the requirements that he or she

---

[41]The words "super-rich" in the title of Lundberg's book refer to a very different group—those with wealth of $75 million or more—from the group termed super-rich by Smith (1969). See above, paragraph 29.

[42]The 1970 survey actually collected information on incomes for 1969 whereas the data on assets are for 1970. The publication cited is chiefly concerned with the latter, but is rather misleadingly entitled *Incomes, Assets and Indebtedness of Families in Canada, 1969.*

should have a residence in close proximity to the non-respondent, have a similar income, be of the same sex and in the same age-group, have similar "labour force status" and the suchlike (Statistics Canada, 1973, p. 176). Slightly different procedures were used for home-owners who refused to reveal the market value of their homes or the amount owing on their mortgages. For business assets, no such assigning was possible, so that tables relating information on these include a category of "not ascertained".

47   The assets which were covered by the 1970 survey were as follows:

1   Cash
2   Bank deposits
3   Other (savings) deposits
4   Government of Canada bonds
5   Other bonds
6   Publicly traded stock
7   Shares in investment clubs
8   Other financial assets
9   Miscellaneous (e.g. loans to others)
10   Homes
11   Vacation homes
12   Other real estate
13   Automobiles
14   Business/Professional interests
15   Insurance, pensions, etc.

Which is, as we have already mentioned, a much more comprehensive list than that used in earlier surveys. The 1956 survey, for example, covered only items 2–5, 8 and 9, while the 1959 survey added item 10. The major omission from this list is undoubtedly consumer durables (except, of course, for automobiles which are included separately). Their exclusion, given that they represent one of the more widely-held or "popular" assets, will cause the resulting distribution of wealth to appear more unequal than it actually is. This is clear from the decile shares derived from the 1970 survey which are given by Podoluk (1970, p. 212). The bottom 40% is shown as holding only 0·4% of total wealth, and the bottom 20% has a net indebtedness equal to 0·9% of total wealth. There can be little doubt that this is an exaggeration of the true position, and that it can largely be explained by the fact that the value of consumer durables, probably the only wealth held by these groups, has not been included. Data on liabilities in the 1970 survey were collected under the following headings:

1   Charge accounts, instalment debt
2   Secured bank loans
3   Other collateral bank loans
4   Home improvement loans
5   Other bank loans
6   Loans from consumer loan companies
7   Credit Union loans
8   Other institutional loans
9   Miscellaneous debts and loans
10   Mortgage debts on homes
11   Mortgage debt on vacation homes

Again this is a fuller definition of indebtedness than that used in earlier surveys, although the differences between surveys are noticeably less than for assets.

48 As with all sample surveys, the estimates derived from this particular sample are subject to sampling error and non-sampling error, the latter including such aspects as non-response. In Section II.2 above we discussed the work of Ferber *et al.* (1969a, 1969b) on non-response in the Survey of Financial Characteristics of Consumers in the USA. They found evidence of significant error associated with non-response; when the report of the 1970 Canadian Survey says therefore that "it is hoped that no serious non-response bias exists in the estimates" (Statistics Canada, 1973), it is clear that the remark is tinged with a certain degree of unfounded optimism. Podoluk (1974), on the other hand, who has brought together the results of the four surveys in an analysis of the distribution of wealth in Canada, is rather more circumspect. As she notes, "The distribution of most types of assets is more highly skewed than that of the income distribution, so that samples designed to measure the overall income distribution with reasonable reliability may be inadequate for the measurement of asset holdings" (1974, p. 206). She refers to the work of Ferber *et al.,* and points to the likelihood that in the Canadian surveys, as elsewhere, "non-reporting of asset holdings may be a greater source of under-estimation . . . than under-reporting of values" (1974, p. 208). As we perhaps might suspect, "popular" assets are measured with greater accuracy in the Canadian surveys, these assets being precisely those with less skewed distributions. Also, even for an asset like savings deposits, smaller deposits (less than $10,000) seem to have been fairly well reported, whereas less than half of deposits held in accounts of $10,000 or more were reported on the basis of comparison with independent known totals from banking statistics. Overall, "survey coverage appears to be in the area of 50% or so" (1974, p. 208).

49 The whole issue of the reliability of the estimates of the distribution of wealth in Canada, derived from the 1970 Survey of Consumer Finances, including in particular the questions of non-random non-response and under-reporting, has been investigated by Davies (forthcoming). He notes, for example, that the 1970 survey estimates are usually lower than estimates from other sources, although the degree of under-estimation varies widely. Some of his results are reproduced here as Table 2. He then attempts to establish the relative contributions to this under-estimation of sampling error, differential response and under-reporting. The first of these is demonstrated to be relatively unimportant, on the basis of a Monte Carlo exercise. A correction for differential response has little effect but the third factor, and specifically complete non-reporting by some respondents, is shown to be very important. When this and the omission of consumer durables and insurance equity are taken account of, a significant increase in the percentage shares of top wealth-holders results. The share of the top 5%, for example, increases from 39·2% to 45·7%, and that of the top 10% from 53·1% to 59·8%. We make use of Davies' re-estimated wealth distribution, and of the unadjusted distribution presented in Podoluk (1974), in Section IV below.

24

TABLE 2
DEGREE OF CANADIAN SURVEY UNDER-ESTIMATION
(SELECTED ASSETS), 1970

Cash and chequing accounts..	53%
Savings accounts and Canada Savings Bonds	54%
Other bonds	78%
Shares	80%
Business equity	18%
Owner-occupied and vacation homes	0
Other real estate	49%
Automobiles	0
Total assets	34%

Source: Davies (forthcoming, Table III).

50   The above virtually exhausts the available published information on assets in the 1970 Survey of Consumer Finances, and, therefore, the available sources of estimates of the distribution of wealth in Canada. We should however briefly mention that the article by Podoluk (1974) also contains an appendix by Emmerson on estimating personal sector aggregate wealth-holdings. These totals are, of course, used to make estimates, such as that cited in paragraph 48, that survey coverage is of the order of 50%. Emmerson notes that, since information on assets and liabilities in the personal sector is based on the records of institutions, they are "derived residually, and the quality of the estimates for the sector depends on the quality of the data available for the other sectors" (1974, p. 217). The quality of these data in Canada in some cases requires improvement, and these deficiencies will, it is hoped, be overcome when official national balance sheet data begin to appear. Although work on this has started, it will be some considerable time before the data are produced; in the meantime research on the distribution of wealth has to rely on the less reliable "*ad hoc* efforts" (1974, p. 217).

IV   A COMPARISON OF ESTIMATES OF THE DISTRIBUTION IN THE USA, THE UK AND CANADA

IV.1   Previous work

51   As a prelude to the presentation and comparison of more recent estimates of the distribution of wealth in the USA, the UK and Canada, we discuss first the work of Lampman (1962) and Lydall and Lansing (1959) who contrasted the distributions of wealth in the USA and Great Britain. No work exists on differences between the distribution in Canada and the UK, for reasons which were made clear in the previous section.

52   Lampman's attempts at a comparison are quite crude as he himself notes, in the main because the distribution in the USA is "built up from very few clues" (1962, p. 212). As we noted earlier, in paragraph 25, he is also concerned about the different mortality multipliers used, but his assessment that "we have

undoubtedly understated the difference [in inequality] between the two countries" (1962, p. 212n) may be incorrect since the effect of lower multipliers in the case of the British estimates is likely to imply a falsely high estimate of the share of top wealth-holders rather than a falsely low one. Lampman first compares the upper tails of the two distributions using the figures estimated for Britain by Langley (1950, 1951), and the difference is quite striking. In 1946–47 the top 1·5% of adults in Britain owned 53% of total wealth, while in 1953 the top 1·5% of adults in the USA owned only 27% of total wealth (1962, p. 211). Lampman then extends the comparison to the complete distribution (although the method of doing so is rather *ad hoc*) and presents Lorenz curves which confirm the much greater inequality in Britain (1962, p. 212). For example, the proportion of wealth owned by the bottom 50% of the adult population in the USA is roughly the same as that owned by the bottom 75% in Britain; the share of the top 2% in Britain is by contrast approximately equal to the share of the top 10% in the USA. As Lampman notes, a similar picture emerges from a comparison of the results of sample surveys. This latter comparison is one which Lydall and Lansing (1959) make, and we quickly review their findings before proceeding to more recent figures.

53   Lydall and Lansing contrast the findings of the 1954 Oxford Savings Survey in Britain, and the 1953 Survey of Consumer Finances in the USA. They suggest that "so far as the available evidence permits us to judge, the tendency towards understatement . . . is very similar" in the two surveys (1959, p. 59); this statement refers to both the proportion of total assets covered in the surveys and the extent of non-response on included assets. The results imply that, in the USA, in 1953, nearly 85% of spending units had positive net worth, while in Britain the comparable figure was only 66%. The Lorenz curves for the two countries' distributions again highlight the much greater inequality in Britain,[43] and the differences are sufficiently great that "it is impossible to believe that they do not reflect a real underlying difference" (1959, p. 61). Lydall and Lansing offer the conclusion, however, that "countries with such similar income distributions are unlikely to retain permanently such large disparities in the distribution of property" (1959, p. 67). In the remaining paragraphs we assess whether the eighteen years since Lydall and Lansing wrote this have seen any significant reduction in the differences between the USA and Britain; we also extend the comparison to Canada.

IV.2   Estate multiplier estimates in the UK and the USA

54   The work of Natrella (1975), Smith (1974) and Smith and Franklin (1974) in the USA, and of Atkinson and Harrison (1978a) and the Royal Commission (1975, 1976, 1977) in Britain,[44] provides a ready source of estate multiplier estimates for these two countries. Many problems of comparability exist, but the most obvious one (and possibly the most important quantitatively) is that figures for the distribution of wealth in the USA are for the top 1% of the total

---

[43]Interestingly, the evidence presented by Lydall and Lansing on the distributions of income in the USA and Britain suggests that, in marked contrast to wealth, there is little difference between the two countries.

[44]Only British figures for 1974 and later include Northern Ireland so that, although we have used UK in the title of Section IV, the estimates all relate to Great Britain.

population while British figures are only for the adult population. In consequence, Natrella's figure for the share of the top 1% in the USA in 1972 of 30·3% of net worth (1975, p. 20), which at first glance is slightly higher than the Royal Commission's figure of 28·1% for the UK in the same year, converts to around 26% when the adult population alone is considered.

55   The estimates for the USA are typically not very comprehensive, because of the limited coverage of the estate tax, and Natrella, for example, reports only the share of all top wealth-holders and the share of the top 1%. Smith and Franklin similarly confine their analysis to the top 0·5% and 1%, so that in what follows we too only consider these highest groups, and do not examine the lower part of the distribution. This disadvantage of the USA figures is more serious in earlier years than for the most recent estimates, of course, because inflation has drawn an increasing proportion of the dying into the estate tax net. For instance, between 1953 and 1972, the estimate of the number of people with gross wealth in excess of $60,000 has increased from a little under 2 million to nearly 13 million, the latter figure representing slightly more than 6% of the total population, or nearly 10% of the adult population.[45]

56   We begin our comparison of the distributions of wealth implied by the estate multiplier method by presenting, in Table 3, various estimates of the shares of top wealth-holders in the USA and the UK for the most recent year for which figures for both countries are available, 1972. It is immediately evident that differences still exist between the USA and Britain in the concentration of personal wealth, but that there is also a substantial discrepancy between different figures for Britain. Both the Royal Commission, and Atkinson and Harrison make a variety of estimates based on different assumptions, and those used in Table 3 are the closest approximation, for each source, to the USA figures. However there are differences in the assumptions underlying the two sets of estimates and it is hence important to consider which of the British figures provides a better comparison to the degree of concentration estimated for the USA by Natrella.

---

[45]For the USA, adult is defined here as aged 20 and over, since this is the nearest we can approximate to 18 and over (as used in the UK figures) given the population figures published in United States Government (1977, p. 217). The effect of the different definitions for the UK and the USA is unlikely to hinder seriously our comparisons however. Atkinson and Harrison show, for example, that the British estimates are sensitive to the definition used, but the effect is relatively small when the group considered is the top 1% (1978a, p. 126). From the results we can see that the lower is the age used to define an adult, the higher is the percentage share of the group under consideration, so that to the extent that there is an effect, it will overstate the share of top wealth-holders in the UK relative to that in the USA. This is confirmed by estimates which Natrella supplied to the Royal Commission in correspondence. For 1972 he calculates the share of the top 1% in the USA at 26·5%, where adult is defined as aged 18 and over, which compares with a figure of 25·8% which we have estimated.

27

TABLE 3

SHARES OF TOP WEALTH-HOLDERS, USA AND BRITAIN, 1972

Country	Estimates of	Share of top	
		1%	5%
USA	Natrella	25·8%	45·3%
Britain ..	Royal Commission	28·1%	53·9%
Britain ..	Atkinson and Harrison	32·0%	57·2%

Notes:
The USA figures are log-linear interpolations of percentages of adult population and total net worth calculated from Natrella (1975, Table 4). The British figures are from Royal Commission (1975, Table 34) and Atkinson and Harrison (1978a, Table 6·5), and, as explained in paragraph 57, the assumptions on which the respective estimates are based differ to some extent.

57   The estimates by the Royal Commission for Britain are based on wealth-holdings derived from estate duty figures and then adjusted to balance sheet totals. In other words, using asset composition data, the amount of each asset which is captured in the estate duty estimates is first calculated, and then the difference between the balance sheet total and this estimate is allocated to holdings of both the included and excluded populations,[46] the allocation depending on the nature of the asset.[47] The estimates are the "series C" figures from the Royal Commission report, which are described as being based on an estimate of "aggregate marketable wealth" (1977, p. 87). They do not therefore include the value of occupational pension rights (series D) or state pension rights (series E), but do improve on the series B figures which make no allowance for the wealth of the excluded population or for any other wealth missing from the statistics.[48] The figures from Atkinson and Harrison differ from those of the Royal Commission in that adjustments are only made for the wealth of the excluded population, so that wealth missing from the estate returns and problems of valuation are ignored. The method followed in making the adjustment is basically the same as that adopted by the Royal Commission, except that only part of the difference between the estate duty estimate for each asset and the balance sheet total is allocated to the excluded population, the remainder being ignored. The proportion actually allocated is varied to generate a range of estimates, and those used in Table 3 are based on assumption B3, which is an

---

[46]The included and excluded populations are respectively the population estimated from the estate multiplier method and the remainder of the adult population.

[47]The full details of the allocation for each asset are described in Royal Commission (1975, pp. 237–39).

[48]Series A is the unadjusted Inland Revenue series which ignores the existence of the excluded population.

intermediate allocation between B2, described as a "lower bound to concentration" where "wealth is allocated as far as is reasonable to excluded population", and B4, an "upper bound" (Atkinson and Harrison, 1978a, pp. 85–86). Atkinson and Harrison also separately make a fuller set of adjustments which might be regarded as closer to those made by the Royal Commission, although interestingly this raises, rather than lowers, the share of the top 1%, to 34·7% (1978a, p. 123). It seems therefore that the difference between the two British estimates represents a basic difference in approach to the whole question of allocation, rather than one which can be explained by which items of missing wealth are included, and which are excluded.

58 This still leaves outstanding the question of which of these sets of estimates is based on closer assumptions to those used to derive the USA figures. The first point to note, of course, is that there are a number of ways in which *all* USA estimates differ from *all* British estimates, but the effects of these differences are discussed more fully below, when we attempt an assessment of what part, if any, of the discrepancy between USA and British estimates can be explained by differences in the basic method applied in each case. The USA figures are adjusted to an aggregate net worth from balance sheet information, with all the excess being allocated to the excluded population. This appears, at first glance, to suggest that the resulting estimates are closer in approach to those of Atkinson and Harrison. This view is incorrect to the extent that the size of the excluded population is much larger, as a proportion of the total adult population, in the USA than in Britain, but since the USA adjustment adds nothing to wealth-holdings within the top 1% or 5%, this is not too serious a problem. In what follows we therefore consider only the figures from Atkinson and Harrison, although it will be worthwhile if the reader bears in mind that the Royal Commission estimates typically suggest a lower degree of concentration.

59 Next then, we must turn our attention to a consideration of how much of the difference between shares of the top 1% of 26% and 32%, and shares of the top 5% of 45% and 57%, can be explained as a consequence of differences in the different applications of and adjustments to the estate multiplier method. These have already been mentioned in Section II, which discussed the nature of the estate statistics in the USA and the estimates based on these; the most important in terms of their quantitative impact on the estimates are the use of higher multipliers than the social class multipliers generally used in Britain, and the valuation of life insurance policies, which are valued far too highly in the estimates of Atkinson and Harrison. Additionally, the fact of allocating the whole of the difference between balance sheet and estate totals to the excluded population, as is done in the USA figures, is potentially of importance when comparing the estimated distributions of wealth in the two countries. Taking each of these in turn, the use of higher multipliers has been investigated by Atkinson and Harrison (1978a, ch. 3). They show that, when *all* excess wealth is allocated to the excluded population, higher multipliers *always* cause the Lorenz curve to shift outwards, thereby raising the shares of the top wealth-holders. This can be confirmed by comparing the results of Smith and Franklin (1974) and Natrella (1975) for 1969. The former use lower multipliers and the implied share of the top 1% of all adults is 23·6%, compared to 25·1% calculated

from Natrella's figures.[49] The implication of this for the comparison between the USA and Britain is that Table 3 would reveal a greater difference between the two countries if the multipliers used to derive the USA estimates were reduced to a level which would make them equivalent to those used by Atkinson and Harrison.

60   The life insurance adjustment to the USA estimates is also one which reduces the difference between the USA and Britain from what it would be if the valuation method were the same in both cases. This is evident from Atkinson and Harrison (1978a, Table 4·7) who show that reducing life policies from the sum assured value to the surrender value increases the shares of the top groups. The reason is, of course, that life insurance is a very widely held asset, so that reducing its value increases concentration quite considerably. The quantitative importance of adjusting to surrender values is of the order of one-tenth of the share of the top 1%, according to Atkinson and Harrison, so that this could increase the share of the top 1% in the UK to around 35%. The impact of adjusting for the different multipliers will likely be less significant, but this, even taking account of the fact that a reduction in the UK figure would result from allocating all rather than only part of the excess wealth to the excluded population, suggests that the share of the top 1% in the USA is about two-thirds of that in Britain,[50] and the share of the top 5% is perhaps around four-fifths of the British figure.[51]

61   Before going on to introduce Canada into the discussion, it is possible to use the estimates of Smith and Franklin (1974) and Atkinson and Harrison (1978a) to compare two time-series of shares of the top 1%. Smith and Franklin (1974, Table 1) give figures for 1953, 1962, 1965 and 1969, and Taussig (1976) cites preliminary figures for 1972, also estimated by Smith, which are consistent with these.[52] The shares of the top 1% of the adult population derived from these are given in Table 4, together with estimates for Britain from Atkinson and Harrison (1978a, table 6·5). The latter are calculated on the same basis as those in Table 3 above, while Smith's figures are broadly equivalent to Natrella's 1972 estimates, except that the multipliers used are not as high. The figures seem to suggest a falling share in Britain but a virtually unchanging share in the USA. In fact this impression is partly spurious since, as both Atkinson and Harrison and the Royal Commission have noted, the series for Britain is

---

[49]This comparison is complicated by the fact that Natrella's figure for total net worth in 1969 of $2,716 billion is about 10% lower than Smith and Franklin's. We therefore interpolated the shares of the top 1% in each case and then standardised by expressing the implied wealth of the top 1% from Smith and Franklin as a percentage of Natrella's net worth figure. The shares expressed as percentages of Smith and Franklin's net worth are of course lower: 21·3% and 22·7%.

[50]This increases to three-quarters if the Royal Commission's estimates are used.

[51]The definition of adult used in the USA estimates (20 and over, rather than 18 and over as in the British figures) will work in the opposite direction to the other factors mentioned, but its impact is likely to be relatively small by comparison with these other factors.

[52]The 1953 figure is actually that originally estimated by Lampman (1962). Subsequent figures are all estimated by Smith on a comparable basis to that of Lampman. As we noted in paragraph 30, the 1969 figure differs from that given in Smith (1974) because of the desire to maintain consistency over time.

affected by the much more restricted coverage of the estate data prior to 1960. Atkinson and Harrison estimate that the shift in the series between 1959 and 1960 because of the increased coverage could be of the order of 7 percentage points (1978a, p. 166) so that the estimates for 1953 and 1958 would be reduced to 37% and 34% respectively. However, a more reasonable assessment of the shift is given as roughly half the 7 percentage points (1978a, p. 167) so that there is still some decline in Britain over the years 1953–1972 but none in the

TABLE 4

SHARES OF TOTAL WEALTH OF THE TOP 1% OVER TIME, USA AND BRITAIN

	1953	1958	1962	1965	1969	1972
USA	23·9%	23·2%	23·1%	25·1%	21·3%	22·7%
Britain	43·5%	40·9%	31·9%	33·3%	31·3%	32·0%

Notes:

The USA figures are calculated by log-linear interpolation from Smith and Franklin (1974, table 1) and Taussig (1976, table 4). The British figures are from Atkinson and Harrison (1978a, table 6·5).

USA. On the other hand it is clear that the decline was at an end by 1962 and from then until 1972 the USA figure stays at a little over two-thirds of that for Britain. In this case, it is worth bearing in mind that Smith's multipliers are lower than Natrella's so some part of the discrepancy associated with differing multipliers between the USA and Britain is allowed for in Table 4. Additionally, Smith and Franklin suggest a downward bias from "best" estimates of 10–15% because of the desire to produce a consistent series (1974, p. 163), although this is arguably true of the British estimates also. For example, the life insurance valuation is still a sums assured basis for Britain against a surrender value basis for the USA, so that adjustment for this would widen the gap between the figures for the two countries. Whether this is as true for 1962 as it is for 1972 is uncertain however, since life insurance has not always been the important "popular" asset it is today.

IV.3   The distribution in Canada, the UK and the USA

62   Since the only information on the distribution of wealth in Canada is that available from sample surveys, while in the USA and the UK the major source is the estimates from use of the estate multiplier method, any comparison of the three countries together is particularly difficult. To make matters worse, in the case of all surveys, all that is published in the reports is the frequency distribution, that is, the proportion of the population in each asset range; no data are included on the average holding in each range from which to estimate the percentage of total wealth held by people within the range. Podoluk (1974) however does give decile shares of assets of all family units, ranked by size of asset-holding, for 1970, and this information is reproduced in Table 5. Unfor-

31

tunately Podoluk's figures do not allow a direct comparison with Table 3 since, apart from any problems of comparability between estate multiplier and sample survey estimates, Table 3 is only confined to the shares of the top 1% and 5%. It is possible to go further down the estimated distribution in Britain at least, and the top 10%, for example, in 1970 owned 69.4% of total wealth according to the figures of Atkinson and Harrison (1978a, table 6.5). The share of the top 20% is estimated at 84.9%, so that on this evidence the distribution in Canada appears appreciably less concentrated than in Britain. This is confirmed by Davies (forthcoming) who has used unpublished data to calculate the shares of the top 1% and 5% implied by the 1970 survey. These are respectively 18.0% and 39.1%[53] both significantly lower than Atkinson and Harrison's British figures for 1970 (equivalent to those for 1972 in Table 3) of 30·1% and 54·3% (1978a, Table 6·5), and lower even than the 1972 USA figures in Table 3. The Canadian figures are, however, subject to strong qualifications. In the first place they are derived from sample surveys with all the accompanying problems.[54] Additionally, the results cover households rather than individuals. Failure to make allowances for these, and other, differences between the Canadian estimates and those of the USA and the UK based on estates, could lead to false conclusions on the relative degree of wealth inequality in the three countries.

TABLE 5

THE DISTRIBUTION OF WEALTH IN CANADA, 1970

Top ..	10%	20%	30%	40%	50%	60%	70%	80%	90%	100%
Own..	53·9%	71·6%	83·4%	91·6%	96·8%	99·6%	100·7%	100·9%	100·9%	100·0%

Notes:

The Table is part of Table 6 from Podoluk (1974, p. 212). The figures in some cases exceed 100% because of the net indebtedness of those in the lower tail of the distribution. The distribution is one of households, rather than individuals. The high proportion of units for whom net worth is negative probably reflects, at least to some extent, the omission of consumer durables other than cars from the survey's definition of net worth, discussed above in paragraph 47.

63 In view of these problems it might be considered preferable to concentrate our attention on sample surveys of households in the USA and Britain, making adjustments where necessary for the fact that the years covered by the various surveys are sometimes quite far apart. However, a further problem is that reports of surveys in all countries show a marked reluctance (perhaps justifiably) to publish the estimated distribution of wealth, preferring instead to discuss such aspects as composition of portfolios, differences among age-groups and the suchlike; additionally the distribution, if it is published, is frequently by size of income rather than wealth. As an alternative we make use of the re-estimated shares of the top 1%, 5% and 10% in Canada in 1970, given by Davies (forthcoming); the nature of the re-estimation is discussed in paragraph

---

[53]Davies also gives a figure for the share of the top 10% of 53·1% which is lower than that given by Podoluk (53·9%). He offers no explanation of the discrepancy.

[54]It is interesting however to note that, after some juggling, Lampman concludes that the figures from the Survey of Consumer Finances for 1953 are close to those he derives using the estate multiplier method (1962, p. 197). This is not the experience of Davies (forthcoming) whose work is discussed above, in paragraph 49.

49 above. In what follows these are compared with estate-based estimates for the USA (1969) and Britain (1970), taken from the same sources as those used in Table 3.

64   The relevant estimates for Canada, the USA and the UK are given in Table 6, and illustrated in Figure 1.   For the USA, Natrella gives figures for 1969 which allow us easily to estimate shares of the top $6\frac{1}{2}\%$ adult wealth-holders. Taking these as the closest available to 1970, the shares of the top 1% and 5% can be interpolated, as can the share of the top 10%, given that the share of the top 100% is necessarily 100%. The UK figures are for 1970 and are taken from Atkinson and Harrison (1978a, Table 6·5), and the Canadian estimates are those of Davies (forthcoming Table XII). The survey figures for Canada, before re-estimation by Davies, are given in parentheses. The differences between the USA and Britain are broadly equivalent to those noted on the basis of Table 3,

FIGURE 1

**LORENZ CURVES FOR THE DISTRIBUTION OF WEALTH
CANADA, USA AND BRITAIN**

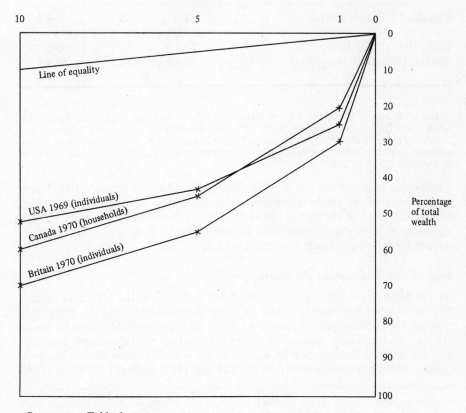

Sources: see Table 6.

33

and the share of the top 10%, not given in Table 3, confirms the trend of significantly lower shares of top wealth-holders in the USA than in Britain. The figure for the share of the top 1% in Canada is below that of the USA while those for the top 5% and 10% in Canada exceed the USA figures. Compared with Britain, however, Canada's Lorenz curve, like the USA's, is closer to the line of equality. Some part of the difference between Canada and the UK may be explained by the fact that the Canadian figures are for family units and unattached individuals, since an adjustment for this would probably increase the percentage shares somewhat. The likely increase is, however, small relative to the differences in Table 6. Atkinson and Harrison, for example, argue, on the basis of experimentation with UK estimates for 1970, that the increase in this case "would not exceed 5 percentage points, and may well be considerably smaller" (1978a, p. 247).

TABLE 6

THE DISTRIBUTION OF WEALTH, CANADA, USA AND BRITAIN

Country and year	Share of the top		
	1%	5%	10%
Canada, 1970 (households)	21·6% (18·0%)	45·7% (39·2%)	59·8% (53·1%)
USA, 1969 (individuals)	25·1%	43·7%	53·0%
Britain, 1970 (individuals)	30·1%	54·3%	69·4%

Notes:

The USA figures are adapted from Natrella (1975, Table 4); the Canadian figures are taken from Davies (forthcoming, Table XII) and the British figures from Atkinson and Harrison (1978a, Table 6·5). The Canadian figures in parentheses are the unadjusted survey estimates, given by Davies (forthcoming); the share of the top 10% differs from that calculated by Podoluk (1974, p. 212).

Finally, the share of the top 10% in the USA is likely to be understated as a consequence of the crude interpolation used to derive it,[55] but it nevertheless seems likely that, at the end of the 1960s, the shares of top wealth-holders were significantly higher in Britain than in either the USA or Canada. The final part of this study considers why this might be.

IV.4 Factors influencing the distribution

65 Reports of research on the distributions of wealth in the USA and Britain have sometimes commented briefly on possible explanations for the differences between the two countries. Lampman (1962), for example, citing work by Straw (1956), who made a comparison of the 1953 USA Survey of Consumer Finances and the Oxford Savings Survey for the same year, mentions the higher proportion of the population aged over 60 in Britain (16% against 12% in the USA)

---

[55]For example, the UK figure for the top 10%, if it were interpolated on the same basis as the USA figure, would be 62·5% instead of the actual figure of 69·4% given in Table 6.

and the greater tendency for families in the USA to own their own homes. This latter aspect is also stressed by Lydall and Lansing (1959) who point in particular to the fact that many more lower-paid workers in the USA than in Britain were home-owners in the 1950s, and remark that, "in respect of property owner-ship there is more difference between the social classes in Britain than in the USA" (1959, p. 64). Associated with this, of course, is the much greater pre-valence of publicly owned rental housing in Britain; in the 1950s, for example, about 20% of the total housing stock was publicly owned in Britain, while in the USA the figure was very small at about 1%.

66   Assuming, for the moment, that these factors are important, it is relevant to note that some of these differences still persist today, and that similar contrasts exist between Britain and Canada. In 1971, 13% of the total British population was aged over 65 and a further 37% was aged between 45 and 64. In Canada the equivalent figures were 8% and 19% and, in the USA, 10% and 20%, so that there is clear evidence of a British population much older than that in Canada and the USA. Turning to the question of housing tenure, in Britain in the early 1970s the proportion of the total stock which was owner-occupied had risen to over 50%. In the USA the proportion of all occupied units which were owner-occupied in 1970 was 63%, and in Canada the figure was only slightly lower— 60% in 1971. In this case then, Britain has moved much closer to the USA, although it is relevant to bear in mind that this increase merely offsets the decline of the private rented sector. Publicly-owned rented accommodation is still very important in Britain (particularly in Scotland where the extent of owner-occupation is correspondingly lower at around 30% in 1971), and this latter feature is regarded by some as a more powerful explanation of some part of the differences between the countries' distributions of wealth.

67   As yet, of course, we have not established that either of the factors we have been discussing is actually of relevance to the distribution. Furthermore, it is possible that the distributions might otherwise diverge by even more—in other words, the factors might be relevant to the distribution but, if they were adjusted for, would increase the differences, or leave them relatively unchanged. For example, the effect of the size of the privately-owned sector of the housing stock is sometimes difficult to pin down precisely.

68   It is undoubtedly true that owner-occupation in Britain has moved closer to the position in the USA; it is probably safe to presume that this is also true in Canada;[56] furthermore, the distribution of wealth in Britain is less con-centrated today than in the 1950s, whereas Table 4 suggests virtually no change in concentration in the USA. There does appear, then, to be some basis for the belief that an upward trend in owner-occupation has an equalising effect on the distribution of wealth. However, Atkinson and Harrison (1978a) have attempted to test for such an effect with inconclusive results. A regression analysis, with the share of total wealth of the top 1% of the adult population as the dependent variable, yields results which admit the possibility, but nothing stronger, than an important explanatory variable is the ratio of "popular assets" (including

---

[56]In fact, compared with 1966, owner-occupation in Canada shows a slight fall in 1971, from 63% to 60%.

housing) to other wealth. From one equation, Atkinson and Harrison suggest that "a rise in the value of owner-occupied housing and consumer durables from 40% to 50% of other wealth would reduce the share of the top 1% by about ½ percentage point", but when a variable measuring the impact of estate duty is introduced "the effect of popular wealth is insignificant" (1978a, pp. 238–40). The Royal Commission, on the other hand, is much more confident about the relevance of this factor. Between 1960 and 1975, the proportion of total wealth accounted for by dwellings (net of mortgages) rose from 17% to 37% as a consequence of increased owner-occupation, together with relatively fast increases in the price of dwellings, and this growth is described by the Royal Commission as "important . . . when considering changes in the distribution of wealth since the early 1960s" (1977, p. 142). Indeed, the *Third Report on the Standing Reference* of the Royal Commission, quoted above, devotes a chapter to the subject of housing, in view of its "considerable and growing importance" (1977, p. 142). A further related factor which may explain part of the difference is that mentioned earlier, the prevalence of publicly-owned housing in Britain. Within Britain, Scotland has an appreciably higher proportion of this type of housing than England and Wales, and it has been suggested that this is one possible factor responsible for the greater concentration of wealth in Scotland, compared with England and Wales.[57] Such an argument relies on the belief that an allocation of some additional amount of wealth should be made to council house owners on the basis of the value of their property rights. Once this is included, however, a number of other assets must also be taken account of, such as state pension rights. We have deliberately steered clear of this contentious area since, even if we were to make some allowance, as the Royal Commission does, for state pension rights,[58] there are no comparable figures for the USA and Canada.

69   Finally, we should ask what other factors might be responsible for the differences in concentration between Britain, on the one hand, and the USA and Canada on the other. Perhaps the most likely one, but one which is certainly just as difficult to quantify as those already discussed, is inheritance. We have already mentioned, in paragraph 43, the work of Barlow, Brazer and Morgan (1966) for the USA, which suggests that, except for the wealthiest individuals, inheritance is not an important determinant of wealth-holdings. Also for the USA, Projector and Weiss (1966) have examined this question. Some of their results are given here as Table 7 and although these give only a poor indication of the importance of inheritance in value terms, it is clear that they broadly support the finding of Barlow, Brazer and Morgan (1966). Turning to Canada, there is less evidence for such a conclusion than exists in the USA. The report of the 1970 survey (Statistics Canada, 1973) does argue that "the role of inheritance is significant only in a few individual cases", and mentions particularly "individuals with very large portfolios" (1973, p. 21). The basis for this observation is not made clear, however, and one is forced to the conclusion that the

---

[57]The higher shares of the top wealth groups in Scotland can be seen in Royal Commission (1975, p. 123).

[58]As one might expect, the effect on the share of the top 1% of including the value of state pension rights is quite dramatic, lowering it from a figure of 25·6% (which includes occupational pension rights) to 17·4% (Royal Commission, 1975, p. 92).

TABLE 7

INHERITED ASSETS IN RELATION TO TOTAL ASSETS, USA, 1962
(% of total consumer units)

Size of wealth	Inherited assets			
	None	Some	Portion of total assets	
			Small	Substantial
$1—$999	95%	5%	5%	*
1,000—4,999	87%	12%	9%	4%
5,000—9,999	82%	18%	12%	6%
10,000—24,999	77%	23%	17%	6%
25,000—49,999	75%	24%	16%	9%
50,000—99,999	74%	24%	12%	12%
100,000—199,999	46%	54%	32%	22%
200,000—499,999	59%	41%	28%	13%
Over $500,000	39%	59%	24%	34%
All units	83%	16%	12%	5%

Note:

Part of Table A32 from Projector and Weiss (1966, p. 148). An asterisk indicates a figure of less than $\frac{1}{2}$%.

report is extrapolating from the findings for the USA of Barlow, Brazer and Morgan (1966) and Projector and Weiss (1966), both of which it cites. Davies (1978) has re-examined the basis for the findings of these sample surveys, and finds, however, that comparison with estate tax records in the USA indicates that surveys detect "only a small part of the total" (1978, p. 31). He estimates the level of inherited wealth as $2\frac{1}{2}$–$3\frac{1}{2}$ times the figures conventionally quoted for the USA, and cites three reasons for this result: the high positive skewness of the distribution of inherited wealth which causes an under-estimate of the sample mean and level of dispersion; under-reporting caused by a variety of factors; and differential non-response with the wealthy families responding less readily than less wealthy families.

70 Research on this question for Britain suggests, in fact, that there is indeed a substantial impact on the wealth of top wealth-holders. In particular the work of Harbury (1962), Harbury and McMahon (1973) and Harbury and Hitchens (1976) has painstakingly traced the estates of fathers of wealthy people who have died, and yields evidence on the proportion of top wealth-holders in one generation who were preceded by top wealth-holders in the previous generation. In a further article, Harbury and Hitchens (1977) summarise the results: "the proportion was a relatively stable two-thirds from the 1920s to the 1960s" but

more recently has declined slightly so that "approximately three-fifths of top male wealth-leavers (leaving over £200,000 in 1973 prices) were preceded by fathers who were at least moderately rich" (1977, p. 125). There are, it must be said, a number of difficulties with this general approach which are documented by the Royal Commission (1975, p. 120) and which Harbury clearly acknowledges. However, it does appear that inheritance has indeed played an important role, and this in spite of increased estate duty rates which were expected to prevent large fortunes from passing largely intact between generations. This conclusion is supported by an interesting investigation of a sample of estates, carried out by the Royal Commission (1977, pp. 166–197). In particular, it finds that the ratio of inherited wealth to total wealth in 1973 was of the order of 20%, and that, taking account of other transmitted wealth such as gifts *inter vivos,* exempt from estate duty if made more than seven years before death, and exempt settled property, the ratio of the total of all transmitted wealth to total wealth was around 25% (1977, Tables 90 and 91). While these results are heavily qualified by the Royal Commission, they are nevertheless in stark contrast to even the re-estimated figures of Davies for the USA. His estimate is that inherited wealth accounted for "about 12% of 1959 household wealth" (1978, p. 29), approximately half the figure calculated by the Royal Commission.[59] We therefore feel it is quite likely that the greater concentration we observe in Britain, compared with the USA and Canada, can be partly attributed to the fact that inheritance continues to feature prominently as a cause of persistent large fortunes.

---

[59]Brittain (1978) also makes estimates of the extent of inherited wealth in the USA, although only as a proportion of the wealth at top percentiles. These ratios are typically much higher than 12%, for example nearly half of the wealth of those at or above the second percentile ($165,000 in 1972), but are not in direct contradiction to Davies' 12% figure. Brittain does not, unfortunately, extend his analysis to the overall impact of inheritance.

CHAPTER 3

THE DISTRIBUTION OF WEALTH IN OTHER COUNTRIES

I INTRODUCTION

71 In the preceding chapter we considered the distribution of wealth in the USA and Canada at some length and made comparisons between these countries and the UK. We now turn to the remaining countries we propose to study: Australia, Belgium, Denmark, France, Ireland, New Zealand, Sweden and West Germany. As we have noted more than once already, we do not feel that an overall comparison such as that offered in Table 6 is possible in the case of this group of countries, so we intend instead to discuss the available estimates in terms of:

(a) the methods used to obtain them; and

(b) the likely sign (but not magnitude) of any difference between them and equivalent UK estimates arising from differences in technique.

72 For convenience we decided to separate the eight countries into four groups. The criterion used was geographical proximity, so that we consider in turn Australia and New Zealand; Denmark and Sweden; Belgium, France and West Germany; and Ireland. There may be an argument for including Ireland with other countries of Western Europe, but unlike the practice in these latter countries, the Irish estimates are derived on a basis quite similar to that used in the UK and can therefore be compared rather more closely with the UK figures, so that we prefer to consider them separately.

II AUSTRALIA AND NEW ZEALAND

73 Both Australia and New Zealand operate estate taxes, which fact suggests that, in principle, estimates of the distribution of wealth can be derived for both countries using the estate multiplier method. In New Zealand official estimates were prepared for a number of years on this basis, and these were published in the Statistical Yearbook. Unfortunately, this practice ceased in 1947 from which time there have appeared only two sets of estate-based estimates, both unofficial: those of Crothers (1975) and Easton (forthcoming). In Australia the estate multiplier method was used over sixty years ago by Knibbs (1918). Since these early estimates, however, there appears to have been no further use of the available estate statistics until the work of Gunton (1971), and it is fair to say that this research, and that of Crothers and Easton in New Zealand, is relatively unsophisticated by comparison with, say, the work of the Royal Commission, or of Smith in the USA.

74 There do not exist any further estimates of the distributions of wealth in these two countries other than the figures derived from the Australian Survey of Consumer Finances and Expenditures of 1966–68. The survey was conducted on behalf of Macquarie University and the University of Queensland by the Survey Research Centre (Private) Limited of Sydney, and the asset data collected is analysed by Podder and Kakwani (1976). No sample survey estimates are

available for New Zealand, and no recent use has been made of the investment income method in either country.

75 In the remainder of this section, and in the other sections of this chapter, we consider in turn the use of the estate multiplier method (where applicable) and the use of other estimation methods. Contrary to our practice in Chapter 2, we do not present the estimates separately from the discussion of the methods used, preferring instead to conclude the latter with details of the former, including an analysis of the direction in which the shares of top wealth-holders might change if adjustments were made to improve comparability with UK figures.

II.1 Estate-based estimates in Australia and New Zealand

76 In Australia the only relatively recent estate-based estimates are those of Gunton (1971) for 1967–68. These are derived from Commonwealth Estate Duty statistics, the valuation for which, Gunton suggests, "cannot be greatly improved on, if at all" (1971, p. 1). The only qualification he adds to this statement concerns the problems caused in the lower tail of the distribution by the estate duty exemption limit, a feature, of course, not peculiar to Australia. Although Gunton's claim seems a little exaggerated—he makes no mention, for example, of the method of valuation used in the case of life policies or pension rights—it is probably fair to say that the valuation is not improved upon by other methods of estimating the distribution of wealth, as we demonstrate below in our discussion of the sample survey results for Australia.

77 The Australian estate duty statistics are presented in age intervals of 10 years, except for the youngest and oldest age groups,[1] and are of course also disaggregated by sex and size of estate. The statutory exemption means that very few small estates appear in the statistics: for instance, the number of recorded estates in the range $1–$9,999 in 1967–68 is 45, while in the range $10,000–$19,999 it is 2,293. In Queensland, however, the State's Succession Duty allows complete exemption only on estates of less than $3,000. Gunton therefore adjusts the Australian data between $4,000 and $19,999 by assuming that the number of estates in Queensland between these amounts is one-seventh of the total for Australia.[2] The mean value of these extra estates is assumed to be the same as the mean of those already in the Australian statistics, and additionally, estimates are made of the number and mean value in the ranges $1–$1,999 and $2,000–$3,999 by extrapolation. The procedure used to perform the extrapolation is a rather arbitrary one: Gunton first distributes the adjusted numbers of estates in the ranges $6,000–$9,999, $10,000–$19,999 and $20,000–$29,999 uniformly across the range[3] to yield the number per $2,000 of the range; pairs the resulting figures with the mean estate size in each range; fits a cubic to these

---

[1] The groups are 0–19, 20–29, . . ., 70–79, and 80 and over.

[2] In 1967 the population and number of deaths in Queensland were both a little over 14% of those in Australia as a whole.

[3] The data for the range $20,000–$29,999 are the unadjusted Australian figures. Between $4,000 and $19,999 the data are adjusted as described above, that is by reference to data for Queensland.

three pairs, plus the pair of values for the range $4,000–$5,999 and, using the estimated cubic, sets the mean estate size at $1,000 and $3,000 to yield estimates of the number of estates in the ranges $1–$1,999 and $2,000–$3,999 respectively.

78   While Gunton's attempts at improving the estate duty statistics between $4,000 and $19,999, and below $4,000, are novel in a number of respects, they nevertheless do introduce possible sources of error. The use of the Queensland data in the former case will not necessarily cause problems, but the assumption that the mean value of recorded estates in Australia also applies to the estates added to the statistics probably overstates the total value of these estates. This is because estates below the exemption limit which are recorded are not generally representative of estates in these ranges, but tend instead to have a significantly higher mean value.[4] The result is that the proportion of wealth held in the lower tail of the distribution is artificially high, and the share of top wealth-holders correspondingly understated. A preferable procedure would surely have been to have used the estate values from the Queensland statistics, although it may be that this information was not available to Gunton.

79   The extrapolation to estate ranges below $4,000 is much more difficult to assess, although a number of points can be made. First, Gunton does not explain his choice of a cubic function for interpolation, nor does he discuss the question of whether the resulting fit is a reliable one. Secondly, the usual practice of using the total population less the population estimated from the estate estimates as a control total for the size of the population excluded from the estimates is not followed here, which would serve as a reliable check on the appropriateness of the adjustments. Finally, it would be of interest to investigate the possibility that alternative data sources, particularly the Australian Survey of Consumer Finances and Expenditures, might shed light on the question of the value of the smaller estates. We return to the question of the population size when we discuss the estimates below.

80   Next we turn to a brief consideration of the mortality multipliers Gunton uses. He begins with the 1960–62 Australian Life Tables, derived from the 1961 Census, extending them forward to 1967 on the basis of the change over that time in age- and sex-specific mortality rates.[5] As Gunton notes, the multipliers derived from life tables are not appropriate for large estates because of the observed correlation between wealth and longevity. He does not, however, use social class mortality rates, for reasons which are not entirely clear,[6] but

---

[4] For example, the 1970 estimates of the distribution of wealth in Britain, prepared by the Inland Revenue, show a mean wealth level of around £3,000 for individuals below £10,000, the exemption limit at that time (Inland Revenue, 1976). Atkinson and Harrison point out however that the maximum possible for all estates below £10,000 is £1,700 per estate (1978a, p. 109).

[5] These rates are deaths per thousand of the estimated population in each age-sex cell at June 30, whereas census mortality rates are averaged over the three year period centred on the census year. As we would expect, "the two move together very precisely" (Gunton, 1971, p. 2).

[6] "I tried adjusting the Australian Life Table mortality rates but the results were unsatisfactory" (Gunton, 1971, p. 3).

instead attempts to find rates from other countries which predict a life expectancy at birth comparable to that known for estates in excess of $100,000 in Australia. Hence, Gunton uses the mortality rates of males in Denmark in 1964 for male estates between $100,000 and $199,999, and those for Sweden in 1963 for estates of $200,000 and over, adjusting the Australian multipliers by the ratio of the Australian rate in 1962 to the appropriate foreign rate.[7] In the case of females, the mortality rates for females in France in 1965 are used to adjust all multipliers applied to estates of $100,000 and over. Gunton's explanation for this procedure is that, in the absence of data on the mortality of top-wealth-holders in Australia, there is no possible alternative. It is difficult to accept however that no information on mortality is available from, say, Australian life insurance companies, which might, at the very least, serve as a check on the adjustments Gunton makes.

81   The only other aspect of the method followed by Gunton which should be briefly mentioned is his treatment of the estates for which age is not stated. He assumes that all males in this category die at 68, and all females at 74, these ages being the respective approximate life expectancies of the sexes. This practice differs from that used in either the USA or the UK estimates,[8] but the reason given by Gunton—that where age is not stated it is usually because it is not known, so that the deceased is likely to be "quite old" (1971, p. 2)—seems quite plausible. Indeed there is no reason at all why those in the "age not stated" category in one country should bear any resemblance at all to those in another country.

82   Having constructed his adjusted estate data and mortality multipliers, Gunton then proceeds to estimation of the distribution of wealth in Australia in 1967–68. The method used differs in a number of respects from that used in, for example, the UK, most notably in the treatment of small estates. Presumably the Queensland Succession Duty statistics which are used by Gunton to estimate the numbers of estates in the lowest estate ranges are not disaggregated by age or sex, so that an overall multiplier is used to estimate the total numbers in these wealth ranges. The need to make such an approximation only serves to reinforce the reservations expressed above, in paragraph 79, about the methods by which the numbers and values of these small estates are estimated.

83   Rather than present the actual figures Gunton has estimated for Australia, we consider next the use of the estate multiplier method in New Zealand before discussing the two sets of estimates together. As we mentioned earlier, there are two sets of estate-based estimates for New Zealand, those of Crothers (1975) and Easton (forthcoming). The former author however "uses the estate duty data provided officially, without any attempts to recalculate in ways which might remove . . . sources of error" (1975, p. 3), in other words, he does not apply mortality multipliers, preferring instead to present the unadjusted estate data itself. The problems of this approach are enormous, since, as Merwin notes, the distribution of estates is "far from being the distribution of wealth

---

[7] No reason is offered for making the correction in terms of the 1962 Australian mortality rates.

[8] See above, paragraph 21.

42

among the living" (1939, p. 12). Neither can one discern anything about trends over time, for changing mortality rates could quite easily nullify the "major change in the pattern of ownership of wealth" which Crothers detects from the raw estate data (1975, p. 7). In what follows we therefore concentrate exclusively on Easton's work.

84   Easton begins by noting the problems for the estate multiplier method arising from the nature of the legislation surrounding the estate tax in New Zealand. For example, gifts *inter vivos* are taxable as part of the estate of the donor only if made within three years of death. This compares with three years in the USA, but seven in the UK before the change to the capital transfer tax. The treatment of jointly-owned family homes is a further example of the way in which wealth is omitted from estate statistics, since an exemption allows part of the value of such property to be transferred without being included in the first spouse's estate. In this case, the New Zealand practice is closer to that followed in the UK than to that in the USA.[9] It is difficult to establish the effect on the estimates of the different practices regarding gifts *inter vivos*,[10] but it seems likely that the second problem mentioned, the exclusion from the statistics of some joint property, will tend to overstate the shares of top wealth-holders. Easton, however, suggests that the magnitude of the overstatement will be slight, since the amount of wealth missed in this way is relatively small.

85   The published details of Easton's use of the estate multiplier method are sparse, a reflection of the fact that he has made few adjustments to the basic method. In particular, stratification of the sample is "by age only" which presumably means that differential mortality between the sexes is ignored, as is the greater life expectancy of wealthier individuals. The only other remark Easton makes about his application of the estate multiplier method is that he assumes no wealth is held by those under the age of 10. In other words, the multiplier for the estates of the youngest age group is derived from mortality rates for those aged 10 and over, unlike the equivalent multiplier in Gunton's use of the method for Australia, which is based on the mortality of all individuals from birth. The effect of such a difference is unlikely to be large however.

86   We turn next to the actual estimates for Australia and New Zealand of, respectively, Gunton and Easton. For Australia, the resulting distribution is summarised by Gunton in a table, reproduced below as Table 8. There are, however, a number of problems with this table as presented. First, it is constructed in terms of the percentage of total estimated wealth-holders, rather than in terms of the total or adult population, a point we raised earlier, in paragraph 79. Secondly, as will have been clear from our discussion in earlier paragraphs, no attempt is made to compare the estimated total wealth figure with that from independent sources such as is done for the UK and USA estimates. Finally, Gunton's table is based on simple linear interpolation, although we have attempted, without success, to use this method to reproduce his figures from the table on which they are based (table 12 in Gunton (1971, p. 9)). We consider these points in reverse order.

---

[9]See paragraph 14 above.

[10]See, for example, the discussion of the subject in Atkinson and Harrison (1978a, pp. 32–33).

TABLE 8

DISTRIBUTION OF WEALTH IN AUSTRALIA, 1967–68, ESTIMATED BY GUNTON

Percentage of estimated total wealth-holders	Percentage of estimated total wealth
Top 50%	91·1%
Top 25%	75·7%
Top 10%	57·0%
Top 5%	41·0%
Top 1%	19·9%

Source: Table 13 in Gunton (1971, p. 9).

87   The linear interpolation, according to our calculations, yields figures for the shares of the top 1%, 5% and 10% of, respectively, 19·9%, 41·1% and 55·2%. If, instead, the more conventional log-linear interpolation is used, the effect is relatively slight, changing the shares to 20·1%, 41·2% and 55·3%. The question of whether the total wealth figure is correct is, however, more serious, raising as it does all the issues associated with allocating missing wealth to different ranges in the distribution. In the concluding pages of his paper Gunton prepares a revised estimate of total personal wealth, adjusted to take account of such features as life insurance, pension schemes, funeral expenses and the suchlike. The result is an increase from $56,523·6 million (the figure used in the construction of the estimates in Table 8 above) to $60,900·2 million. Gunton does not make use of any independent overall balance sheet totals, and no attempt is made to allocate the extra $4,376·6 million. Without more detailed information than we currently have on the nature of estate duty exemptions in Australia, it is difficult to be very precise about the effect on Gunton's estimates of this, and other, missing wealth. It seems unlikely, however, that the shares of top wealth-holders will be significantly reduced, particularly in view of the fact that Gunton has made adjustments for deficiencies at the lower end of the distribution.

88   Finally, we come to the question of the size of the population. Gunton estimates that the number of wealth-holders is 3,964,060, and since the lowest wealth range begins at $1, and the multiplier for the youngest age group is one for those aged 0 to 19, this figure represents the estate estimate of the total population. The total population in Australia in 1967 was in fact 11,810,200 of which 8,350,500 were aged 20 or over (United Nations, 1969). Clearly, therefore, if we re-estimate Gunton's figures in terms of the total adult population aged 20 and over, the shares of top wealth-holders will be significantly higher.[11] The precise effect is shown in Table 9. The top 1% now has 28·7% of total estimated wealth, and all wealth is in the hands of the top 47·5%, the "included population". Before presenting the equivalent UK figures, however, we first discuss and present the estimates for New Zealand of Easton.

---

[11]In the terminology of the Royal Commission or the Inland Revenue, this is equivalent to the change from series A to series B.

TABLE 9

DISTRIBUTION OF WEALTH IN AUSTRALIA AMONG THE
ADULT POPULATION, 1967–68

Percentage of total adult population	Percentage of estimated total wealth
Top 47·5%	100·0%
Top 25%	92·1%
Top 10%	72·5%
Top 5%	56·6%
Top 1%	28·7%

Notes:
   Table calculated from Table 12 in Gunton (1971, p. 9), on the assumption that the proportion of the adult population not covered by the estate estimates has no wealth.

89   In a number of respects Easton's use of the estate multiplier method is more conventional than Gunton's. For example, he deals with that part of the population excluded from the estimates by adopting the procedure used by the Royal Commission in series B, that is, he assumes no one in this group owns any wealth. This causes problems when comparing estimates over time, of course, as Easton notes, since between 1956 and 1966, the two years for which he prepares estimates, the exemption limit rose from $2,000 to $8,000. In what follows, however, we consider only 1966. The results given by Easton for this year are presented here in Table 10, in terms of the adult population, which is defined as those aged 20 and over plus 55,200 juvenile wealth-holders. The only adjustment we have made to Easton's figures is to adopt a log-linear interpolation technique rather than the linear technique he uses.

TABLE 10

DISTRIBUTION OF WEALTH IN NEW ZEALAND AMONG
THE ADULT POPULATION, 1966

Percentage of total adult population	Percentage of estimated total wealth
Top 55·5%	100·0%
Top 25%	84·7%
Top 10%	60·0%
Top 5%	44·5%
Top 1%	18·2%

Notes:
   Table calculated from Table 3·1 in Easton (forthcoming), on the assumption that the proportion of the adult population not covered by the estate estimates has no wealth.

90 Tables 9 and 10 are not immediately comparable because some individuals who would have been treated as members of the excluded population and assigned zero wealth by Easton are included in Gunton's estate estimates and assigned positive wealth as a consequence of his use of the Queensland data in the lower tail of the distribution. However, an adjustment to Gunton's estimates to overcome this would result in higher shares of top wealth-holders, so that, on this basis the distribution of wealth in Australia appears to be appreciably more unequal than that in New Zealand. Additionally, Easton uses mortality multipliers unadjusted for social class, and the results of Atkinson and Harrison (1978a, ch. 3) show that, if such an adjustment were to be made, this would reduce the shares of top wealth-holders in New Zealand, thereby widening still further the gap between the estimates for the two countries. The closest UK estimates to those presented here for Australia and New Zealand are the Inland Revenue/Royal Commission series B figures. In 1966 the share of the top 1% in the UK according to this source is 31·8%, rising very slightly in 1967, not too different from the Australian figure of 28·7% when one takes account of the equalising influence of Gunton's treatment of small estates, but appreciably higher than the New Zealand estimate. However, in view of the fact that the use of the estate multiplier method in both Australia and New Zealand is at a far more rudimentary stage than in the UK, any comparison such as this must be treated very cautiously indeed.

II.2 Sample survey estimates in Australia

91 To the best of our knowledge, no sample survey data exist in New Zealand on the distribution of wealth. In Australia on the other hand, asset data were collected in the Survey of Consumer Finances and Expenditures (SCFE) in 1966–68, and these are analysed by Podder and Kakwani (1976). One interesting aspect of this analysis is an attempt to compare the percentage shares of top wealth-holders in Australia with those estimated for Canada from the 1970 Survey of Consumer Finances, although, as we show below, the conclusion of "much greater inequality of wealth in Canada" (1976, p. 91) is based on survey estimates for Australia which are less reliable than the equivalent results for Canada.

92 The SCFE successfully interviewed 5,459 households for their expenditures on different commodities, and then returned at a later date to collect data on household finances, including information on incomes and assets. Only about 50% of the households participated at this second stage and "2,757 usable questionnaires were obtained" (Podder and Kakwani, 1976, p. 76). No indication is given of the completeness of the households' answers to questions or assets, a consideration which was found to be important in the 1970 Canadian Survey.[12] Additionally, checks which Podder and Kakwani make on the extent of bias due to non-response only compare the successfully interviewed households at each stage: "the number of families originally approached is not known" so that the "response rate at the first stage of the survey cannot be determined" (1976, p. 78). In consequence, the checks carried out only have a limited relevance, besides which it must be said that they arguably reveal very little about the representativeness of the asset data.

---

[12]See above, paragraph 46.

93 The test Podder and Kakwani use is a comparison of the composition of the samples at the two stages in terms of household size and the age of the head of household. They find no significant difference between the samples, except that households with heads aged under 30 are under-represented in the second sample, for which an adjustment is made. This, of course, assumes that non-random non-response is related in some way to either household size or the age of the head of the household, an issue which Podder and Kakwani do not address. By contrast, the practice in the Canadian surveys is substantially more sophisticated, as is the technique used in the SFCC in the USA of over-sampling high income families. Given that these latter surveys still fail significantly to overcome the problem of non-random non-response, we are left with the impression that the asset details in the Australian survey must be very seriously deficient, and thereby appreciably understate the shares of top wealth-holders. To establish the extent of the problem for the SCFE, it would be very interesting, for example, to see an exercise conducted on the survey results similar to that carried out by Davies (forthcoming) on the Canadian survey estimates.[13]

94 The assets which are covered by the Australian survey include:
1 cash and bank deposits
2 homes
3 other real property
4 automobiles
5 surrender value of life policies
6 superannuation
7 shares and securities
8 household appliances
9 unincorporated businesses

In the case of debts, Podder and Kakwani merely note that "all conceivable debt is included" (1976, p. 79) with the exception of debts outstanding on life policies and personal loans obtained from friends. The major difference between the assets listed here and those covered by the Canadian survey[14] is the inclusion in the former of household appliances. The effect of this is however less than it might otherwise be, because not all household appliances or automobiles are included. Only those bought in 1966–67 or on which hire purchase payments were still outstanding were covered by the survey. Nevertheless the decile shares for the Australian distribution, given by Podder and Kakwani (1976, p. 83), show a marked difference in the lower half of the distribution from those for Canada given by Podoluk (1974, p. 212). In the latter case the bottom 40% of households own only 0·4% and the bottom 20% have a net indebtedness, while in the Australian figures the shares of these groups are both positive, and are respectively 8·71% and 0·91%. This difference can almost undoubtedly be attributed to the omission of consumer durables in the Canadian survey.

95 The results of the Australian survey are reproduced here as Table 11, and suggest that, for example, the top 1% owned around 9% of total net worth in 1966. This figure, and the shares of other groups of top wealth-holders, are

---

[13]For details of this, see above, paragraph 49.

[14]See above, paragraph 47.

47

appreciably lower than equivalent shares in any of the countries so far studied, and are also, of course, much lower than Gunton's estimates for Australia, which he derived from estate data and which, as we argued above, probably understate the true position. Our conclusion therefore is that these sample survey estimates appear rather unreliable, so that little purpose is served by any comparison of them with results from other countries.

TABLE 11

THE DISTRIBUTION OF WEALTH IN AUSTRALIA, 1966

	1%	5%	10%	20%	30%	40%
Top ..	1%	5%	10%	20%	30%	40%
Own ..	9·26%	24·57%	36·45%	53·51%	66·11%	76·23%
Top ..	50%	60%	70%	80%	90%	100%
Own ..	84·55%	91·29%	96·26%	99·09%	100·05%	100·00%

Notes:
   The table is calculated from table 8 in Podder and Kakwani (1976, p. 83). The distribution is one of household units, not individuals, and is derived from sample survey data. For reasons outlined in paragraphs 92–95, the figures probably substantially understate the true position.

III DENMARK AND SWEDEN

96   In both Denmark and Sweden, as in Norway, mentioned above in paragraph 3, wealth distribution statistics, derived from wealth tax returns, are published annually in the respective Statistical Yearbooks. Those for Denmark are published in such a way that percentage shares of top holders of (taxable) wealth can be calculated, and in 1971, for example, the share of the top 10% taxable units in total taxable wealth was 63·7%. However the available information in both countries is seriously inadequate (again as in Norway). Spånt notes, for example, that in Sweden the published statistics cover only 5% of all households and only 10% of total household wealth (1978, p. 6). In Denmark a similar picture emerges with, if anything, a still more restricted coverage, since Sandford's study of the taxation of capital in different countries shows Denmark as having an appreciably higher threshold for its wealth tax than either Sweden or Norway (1978, p. 11). In the light of this, it may initially appear odd that we consider Denmark and Sweden in our survey while excluding Norway. The reason is that, unlike the situation in Norway, some further work has built upon the basic tax statistics in these countries although, particularly in the case of Denmark, the outcome is still highly unreliable. Much of this work is discussed by Spånt (1978), who has himself been concerned with improving the Swedish figures.[15] We therefore begin by considering Sweden, and then turn to Denmark, making comparisons between the two countries where possible.

---

[15]Our discussion of Denmark and Sweden is largely based on Spånt's paper, since a copy of the original source for the former country, a paper by Sørensen (1978), was not obtained until this report was almost completed.

97 Spånt describes the method by which the estimates for Sweden are derived as a sample survey which, he suggests, is superior to the alternative of the estate multiplier method. His justification for this claim is that he is able to base the survey on "secret tax records supplied by the tax authorities" (1978, p. 6). He continues that the study therefore covers virtually "the same assets and debts as the estate duty records", but that instead of having to consider "the unrepresentative group of individuals recently deceased" the survey group can be freely chosen. This is indeed a compelling argument, although whether tax authorities in other countries would be as gracious as the Swedes in allowing access to their records is a debatable point.

98 It is difficult to establish precisely the nature of the data collected in the sample survey. It is clear from Spånt's remarks that wealth tax records allow a stratified sample to be assembled which systematically oversamples the rich,[16] but it appears also as if the actual data on assets are drawn from these records, which raises the question of how those exempt from wealth tax are covered by the survey. The reason for believing that the data are tax data is that the study is confined to assets and debts covered by the wealth tax, a restriction which need not be imposed if the data were collected in the field, after identification of the sample from tax records. Alternatively it may be that tax data are supplemented by a survey of households not covered by these data.

99 The survey was conducted in 1975, the basic sample for which numbered about 5,000 households out of approximately 4 million in Sweden overall. The over-sampling in the upper tail was achieved by adding a stratified sample of 3,200 households with net taxable wealth at that time in excess of 200,000 Swedish crowns (about £22,000). All households with net taxable wealth over 10 million crowns were included in the sample, 50% of those in the 5 million to 10 million crown range, and smaller percentages below 5 million crowns. As we have mentioned already, the assets covered by the survey are those which are taxable, although it appears from the list given by Spånt (1978, p. 7) and reproduced in amended form below, that the definition of wealth for tax purposes is quite comprehensive. The types of assets are as follows:

1 Houses and apartments
2 Farms
3 Stocks and inventories
4 Savings accounts
5 Bonds
6 Quoted and unquoted shares
7 Foreign shares
8 Loans
9 Co-operative shares
10 Jewellery
11 Life annuities
12 Consumer durables

---

[16]The nature of this oversampling is discussed in paragraph 99.

The liabilities included are similarly ones which are allowed as liabilities by tax laws. These are listed simply as tax liabilities, mortgages and other liabilities. A number of the assets covered by the Swedish survey are either partially or completely omitted from both the Canadian and Australian sample surveys. Instances of this are jewellery and consumer durables, the latter item being of particular interest. Some of these are typically sold jointly with owner-occupied homes or apartments, so that they appear in this latter category, and not as consumer durables; others, for example, cars, boats, caravans, are durables included as such. In spite of this, however, the number and value recorded understate the true totals according to Spånt, although one feels that this survey probably captures a higher proportion of the total value of durables than others we have discussed.

100 The basic data source in Denmark in similar to that in Sweden, in that tax records are investigated, although Spånt notes that the primary interest of the Danish survey is income rather than assets. The survey Spånt discusses is that for 1975, which sampled 13,600 households out of a total in Denmark of around 2·7 million. The major shortcoming of the survey, compared to that in Sweden, is that no stratification by wealth size was used, so that the "figures on the wealth position of the very rich . . . are rather uncertain" (Spånt, 1978, p. 10). The coverage of assets and debts is broadly comparable to the Swedish survey since the respective countries' tax laws are fairly similar, and the only valuation problem peculiar to the Danish survey mentioned by Spånt is that associated with bonds.

101 In both Denmark and Sweden a substantial revaluation of the tax data is made, the basis for which varies from asset to asset. Spånt's estimates of the distribution of wealth in Sweden incorporate this revaluation, allocating the excess to yield the range of estimates given in the first column of Table 12 below. For Denmark, however, the estimated distribution is in terms of the original "tax values", rather than these adjusted "market values", so that the Danish figures, given in column (3) of Table 12, are presented alongside comparable, but

TABLE 12

THE DISTRIBUTION OF WEALTH IN DENMARK AND SWEDEN, 1975

	(1) Sweden (market values)	(2) Sweden (tax values)	(3) Denmark (tax values)
Percentage shares of:			
Top 1% ..	15–17%	20%	25%
Top 5% ..	28–35%	42%	47%
Top 10% ..	50–55%	57%	63%

Notes:

Figures are for households and are taken from figure 1 and table 4 of Spånt (1978). For a description of the distinction between market and tax values, see paragraph 101.

less comprehensive, estimates for Sweden (column (2)). Spånt argues that the two sets of figures can be compared since the degree of underdeclaration is of a similar size in both countries, although this does require, as he notes, an assumption that the under-declaration also has the same distribution. Surprisingly perhaps, in view of the fact that the Swedish survey oversamples the wealthy, the results suggest that the shares of top wealth-holders are higher in Denmark than in Sweden. As is well known, no comparable data source exists in the UK, and we therefore feel that no purpose is served by making comparisons between the figures in Table 12 and estimates for the UK.

IV BELGIUM, FRANCE AND WEST GERMANY

102 We turn next to a consideration of estimates of the distribution of wealth in countries of Western Europe. The choice of Belgium, France and West Germany was dictated by the belief that figures produced for other countries which would belong in this group are not sufficiently reliable for inclusion in the survey. Hence Holland, like Norway, has a wealth tax and publishes the distribution of taxable wealth but these figures are not discussed here since the high threshold means that a substantial proportion of total wealth is not covered. West Germany is in a similar position, in that estimates of the distribution based on wealth tax returns are published, but are widely recognised as being of little value. However, in this case alternative and superior estimates are available, in addition to which further work is currently in progress.

103 Neither Belgium nor France has a wealth tax, and both these countries rely heavily on sample surveys for evidence on the distribution. Additionally the results for Belgium use the technique of *la capitalisation des revenus,* that is the investment income method. Just as in West Germany, much research on the distribution in Belgium and France is still at an early stage, and within the next few years it is likely that, in all three countries, the quality of estimates of the distribution will improve significantly.

104 As far as we are aware only one set of estimates for Belgium exists: those for 1969 of Walravens and Praet (1978). The principal method adopted is the capitalisation of tax data on incomes, whereby application of the inverse of the appropriate rate of return to each class of income allows the wealth generating that income to be estimated. This is only carried out for assets yielding a taxable return[17] and, in all, around 77% of the total amount of personal wealth is accounted for in this way. For the other categories of wealth, notably consumer durables, life policies, works of art, jewellery and the like, Walravens and Praet use *ad hoc* methods, "based principally on investigations of expenditures or acquisitions of these assets (budget surveys, etc.)" (1978, p. 1).[18] The use of

---

[17]Walravens and Praet seem to be of the opinion that it is not possible to derive an estimate which includes assets with a zero return. This is not however the case. A weighted mean yield for a particular income or wealth class can be constructed taking account of zero yields, as long as data on asset composition are available which include information on the share of these assets in total wealth for the different classes.

[18]The paper by Walravens and Praet is written in French, and all "direct" quotations from the paper are in fact our own translations.

tax data supplemented by sample survey is a novel approach, and it is interesting to note that the provisional results of a study using the estate multiplier method are "close to those obtained" with this method (1978, p. 3). Nevertheless, like all methods, it has its limitations as Walravens and Praet freely recognise.

105   The first problem they discuss is the fact that coverage of the tax data is not complete. Around 29% of the total number of households do not make a tax declaration, and a substantial proportion of these 29% are pensioner households. In order to take account of these households, many of which may hold a certain amount of wealth, income from wealth of "non-declarants" is estimated as being two-thirds of the income of the top three income classes.[19] A further aspect of the use of tax data is that the resulting distribution will be one for *ménages fiscaux* or tax units, although Walravens and Praet do not unfortunately discuss whether the definition of the household for tax purposes differs from the conventional definition.

106   A further well-known problem with this method of estimation is that of determining the appropriate rate of return with which to capitalise incomes. This is not at all adequately discussed by Walravens and Praet, who merely note that difficulties arise because "the rate of return varies with the income class and the type of wealth" (1978, p. 2) without revealing the source of their data or the method of construction of the appropriate yields. This is particularly unfortunate in view of the fact that the choice of yield is, in certain circumstances, critical to the resulting estimates.[20] Walravens and Praet do mention that the rate of return does not necessarily rise with income, a result which they refer to as "paradoxical" (1978, p. 2). The explanation is, however, quite straightforward: "those with high wealth and high marginal tax rates are likely to choose within a particular category of assets those which have a low taxable return" (Atkinson and Harrison, 1978a, p. 173).

107   The final problem to which Walravens and Praet make reference is that the capitalisation of income yields only the mean wealth amount in each income class. To allocate the total wealth across the class, they therefore assume that it is distributed lognormally, noting that variants on this were tested but were found not to "change significantly the total distribution of wealth" (1978, p. 3). The need for any assumption is questionable, since an acceptable alternative is to proceed with the aggregation implied by the data, and to apply an interpolation routine to find the percentage shares of particular groups in the distribution. Expressed this way it is clear therefore that the use of the lognormal distribution represents an interpolation routine at an earlier stage, although the most common routine used, the log-linear one, actually imposes a piecewise Pareto distribution rather than the lognormal. However, the difference between interpolation techniques is not typically critical where the number of wealth classes is reasonably large.

---

[19] Also, of course, wealth may be missed because of tax evasion.

[20] See, for example, Atkinson and Harrison (1978a, p. 197).

108   As we did in the previous section, we reserve comment on the actual estimates until we have discussed the method of estimation used in all the countries considered in this section; we therefore turn now to work on the distribution of wealth in France. Empirical research on asset-holdings, using data from sample surveys, has been conducted for some time, but it is only recently that the issue of the overall distribution of wealth in France has been addressed. Furthermore, the estimates which are available are still presented in a rather circumspect fashion. Much of the research on the subject is carried out under the auspices of CREP (Centre de Recherche Economique sur l'Epargne), and a recent book by two of the members of this agency (Babeau and Strauss-Kahn, 1977) summarises the results of this work and attempts to put it into an international perspective.

109   The first major surveys in France on household wealth and savings were those conducted in 1967 and 1969 by INSEE (Institut National de la Statistique et des Etudes Economiques). These only sampled households in which the head was salaried or inactive, the self-employed being omitted until later surveys because of "delicate theoretical and practical problems" (L'Hardy and Turc, 1976, p. 4).[21] In 1967 there were approximately 12 million households in the categories covered, representing 80% of the population, and of these, 3,000 were sampled, and 2,300 responded. In 1969 the same 2,300 households were included in the second survey, and 2,000 were successfully interviewed. The results generally tend to be less precise than is required for the purpose of estimating an overall distribution of wealth, often only giving details of what proportion of the households hold specific assets, but not of the amounts held.

110   A third survey was mounted in 1973, more complete than its predecessors in terms of the types of households covered, but not in terms of the degree of detail in the asset information requested. The sample size this time was 7,500 households, of which 5,500 responded, and included households where the head was self-employed, as well as those where he or she was salaried or inactive. On the other hand, "to limit the risks of this new experience" (L'Hardy and Turc, 1976, p. 4) the questionnaire for 1973 was made less detailed than those for 1967 and 1969. In consequence, none of these surveys is really suited to estimation of the distribution of wealth, whereas one conducted in 1975 for CREP has been used for this purpose.

111   This last-mentioned survey is discussed briefly by Babeau and Strauss-Kahn (1977). Like the third INSEE survey, it covered all types of households, with a sample size of 2,800; unlike the INSEE survey, however, attempts were made to over-sample the households which were expected to be the more well-to-do in order to avoid the common problem encountered in sample surveys of these households not responding and generating a bias in the sample. The choice of which groups to over-sample was done on the basis of occupation, although Babeau and Strauss-Kahn do not reveal how this information was obtained in advance of the selection of the sample. A further improvement in the CREP survey over the INSEE surveys is that, for financial assets, reference was made to control totals published by the Conseil National du Crédit, on the basis

---

[21]Again this direct quotation is in fact our translation from the French original.

of which adjustments were made to the survey figures where important under-statements of asset amounts were apparent. Unfortunately, no other details of the survey are given by Babeau and Strauss-Kahn.

112   We turn next, in this section, to Germany. Spånt (1978) suggests that economists and politicians in this country have a special interest in the distribution of wealth, by comparison with most other countries, which he attributes to the effects on assets and debts of wars and hyper-inflation. However the statistical basis for the debate is, he argues, rather weak. The main sources of information are the income and expenditure surveys of 1969 and 1973, and the collection of asset data is a relatively minor purpose of these surveys. The implications of this for the quality of the data are acknowledged by Euler who notes that "the recording of assets in the sample surveys . . . has many deficiencies and gaps" (1978, p. 17). As a result, the official agency responsible for under-taking the sample surveys feels "unable to present an estimate" of the overall distribution of wealth, and instead "attempts of this kind have been made by third parties" (1978, pp. 14–15). The paper by Euler, cited above, is a detailed description of the income and consumption surveys and the problems associated with the asset data from the surveys, and the following few paragraphs lean heavily on its analysis.

113   The sample size for the surveys is approximately 55,000, representing 0·25% of the total number of the 22 million private households. Certain groups are not included in the surveys, for example, foreign households, and people living in institutions. In addition the responses of households with an income in excess of 180,000 DM (about £47,000) in 1973 are not processed "because experience has shown that the number of participating households with such high income does not . . . suffice to make a statistically significant statement" (Euler, 1978, p. 4). This last omission is clearly a serious one, particularly for assets which are disproportionately held by the relatively wealthy, such as company shares. A further problem in the selection of the sample is that participation is volunteered, in that respondents are "recruited". Random sampling was dispensed with because of the high rates of non-response in pilot surveys, and instead representativeness is controlled "by means of a household stratification derived from the annual micro-census" (Euler, 1978, p. 4). This procedure is apparently criticised as being inferior to an asset survey of a random sample survey of households, but, as Euler points out, it has its advan-tages also. In particular, the asset questions are only asked after a number of visits to the household, during which time a "climate of mutual confidence" develops. Additionally, asset information can be checked against information on income from dividends, savings bank accounts and the like, which is recorded at the same time.

114   Perhaps the primary deficiency of the surveys is the limited number of assets covered.[22] Spånt suggests that only 50% of private wealth is captured in the surveys (1978, p. 14) and it is certainly true from Euler's discussion of this problem that substantial amounts of wealth are missing. A particular instance

---

[22]Additionally, the 1969 survey established only broad levels of asset-holdings, according to size classes, whereas the 1973 survey determined absolute amounts.

of this is consumer durables, the purchase of which is regarded as consumer expenditure rather than as a rearrangement of an individual's wealth. Hence, from the point of the surveys, money in a savings account is wealth, but once withdrawn and spent on, say a car, it no longer constitutes an asset. While cars probably comprise a substantial proportion of consumer durables, other items in this category include furniture, paintings, and jewellery, so that overall, as we have seen in other surveys, a significant amount of wealth is surely missed in this way. Among other assets which are not covered by the German surveys are cash holdings and current account balances, and in total, Euler estimates that approximately 80% of all financial assets are captured by the surveys. Although consumer durables are ignored, other physical assets are included, notably land and buildings, and commercial enterprises. However, the 1964 tax values are used in these cases, which means that the estimated value of the assets is substantially below the current market values. These deficiences are likely to be to some extent offsetting, for while the omission of consumer durables will tend to overstate the shares of top wealth-holders, [23] the under-valuation of land, buildings and commercial enterprises will work in the opposite direction. Taken together, our feeling is that the final estimated position will reflect the latter effect more than the former, in addition to which, of course, other problems will contribute to some degree of understatement. In this category, for example, is the omission of the high income households from the sample; furthermore, many of the shortcomings which are common to all sample surveys have a similar effect, as the work of Ferber *et al.* (1969a, 1969b) for the USA and Davies (forthcoming) for Canada has demonstrated.

115 In the remainder of this section we present the figures for the distributions of wealth in Belgium, France and West Germany, which have been estimated using the methods outlined above. For Belgium, Walravens and Praet very conveniently give the cumulative percentage shares for all deciles and for the percentiles within the top decile. This degree of disaggregation is of course made possible by their decision to impose the assumption of a lognormal distribution on the aggregated data. The results are reproduced below in Table 13, and show that the share of the top 1% on this basis was nearly 28% in 1969, while the top 5% owned a little under half of total personal wealth.

TABLE 13
THE DISTRIBUTION OF WEALTH IN BELGIUM, 1969

Top ..	1%	5%	10%	20%	30%	40%
Own ..	27·8%	46·7%	57·4%	70·9%	79·7%	86·1%
Top ..	50%	60%	70%	80%	90%	100%
Own ..	90·8%	94·3%	96·8%	98·5%	99·6%	100·0%

Source:
This table is part of Table 5 in Walravens and Praet (1978, p. 11).

[23]This effect is reinforced by the rather odd decision to include as debts the outstanding hire purchase payments on the consumer durables, while ignoring the assets they represent. On this point, see Euler (1978, p. 10).

While the former figure is quite close to estimated shares of the top 1% in Britain for 1969, the latter figure and the share of the top 10% both appear lower than equivalent estimates for Britain, although whether these comparisons indicate more about the method used by Walravens and Praet or about the actual position in the two countries is very difficult to say. No recent estimates of the *shares* of top wealth-holders in Britain based on the investment income method have been constructed, and probably the only systematic investigation of the method using British tax data concludes rather cautiously that, comparing it with the estate duty method, "the investment income approach gives higher estimates of both numbers and wealth, but . . . it is difficult . . . to reject the hypothesis that the distributions are the same" (Atkinson and Harrison, 1978a, p. 200). Until further work of this type is complete, we can say nothing more on the comparison of the distributions in Belgium and Britain.

116   The estimates of the distribution of wealth in France presented us with several problems since there appear to be inconsistencies both between and within tables in Babeau and Strauss-Kahn (1977). The implied decile shares from the CREP survey of 1975 are presented in their Table 35 (1977, p. 164), but no shares of groups within the top decile are given. In a separate publication, we located figures on the proportion of households in six wealth classes and the proportion of total wealth each owned (Caisse des Dépôts, 1977, p. 21), but the increase in detailed information regarding the distribution within the top decile was slight. We therefore referred to an earlier table, Table 20, in Babeau and Strauss-Kahn (1977, p. 132), which contains information on the asset composition of household wealth by size of wealth. There are 11 wealth classes, and the mean wealth size for each class is presented, together with the number of households in each class and the overall mean wealth. From this information, we reconstructed the implied cumulative distribution, but in so doing found discrepancies between Table 20 in Babeau and Strauss-Kahn (1977) and the figures given by Caisse des Dépôts (1977). In particular, the calculation of the share of total wealth in each wealth class, achieved by multiplying the percentage of households in a class by the mean wealth for the class and dividing by overall mean wealth, suggested that all classes together owned 102·6% of total wealth! Clearly therefore, the overall mean wealth was inconsistent with the class means, and a recalculation of the former yielded a figure of 191,818 Francs, rather than the published figure of 186,800 Francs, a difference too large to be attributable to rounding error. Using the revised overall mean, we then estimated the implied percentage shares once again, and the results of applying a log-linear interpolation routine to these figures is given in Table 14. (A fuller description of the problems we encountered in preparing Table 14 is contained in a brief Appendix to this Chapter.)

117   The figures in Table 14 are not easily interpreted, particularly when taken together with those for Belgium in Table 13. For example, the share of the top 1% in France is quite substantially lower than the share of the same group in Belgium,[24] although the implied Lorenz curves for the countries cross at around the top 20%. The share of the bottom 50% in France is therefore lower

---

[24]Indeed, the French figure is lower than any of those so far discussed with the exception of the estimate of Podder and Kakwani for Australia of 9·3%.

TABLE 14

THE DISTRIBUTION OF WEALTH IN FRANCE, 1975

Top ..	1%	5%	10%	20%	30%	40%
Own ..	12·5%	36·2%	51·7%	71·0%	83·6%	91·8%
Top ..	50%	60%	70%	80%	90%	100%
Own ..	96·3%	98·3%	99·4%	99·6%	99·8%	100·0%

Notes:

This Table is constructed from table 20 in Babeau and Strauss-Kahn (1977, p. 134) after adjustments for inconsistencies in the table. See text, especially paragraph 116 and the Appendix to Chapter 3, for details.

than the equivalent share in Belgium, and is in fact only 3·7% of total wealth, which is very close to the figure of 3·2% in Canada; this latter figure, we have argued, is understated as a consequence of the omission of consumer durables from the Canadian survey, yet these assets are included in the French survey. Unfortunately, insufficient information is available on the CREP survey methods to allow us to suggest the existence of any biases in the estimates for France, so that there is really no further commentary we can offer on them. We do however feel that any comparisons across countries of the extent of wealth inequality which use these estimates must be treated with caution.

118   Finally, we come to the estimates for Germany. Figures for 1969 and 1973 are presented in Mierheim and Wicke (1977), but in view of the fact that absolute asset amounts were only obtained in the 1973 survey, we confine ourselves here to this later year. The percentage shares given by Mierheim and Wicke are only for quintiles, but Table 4 in the paper (1977, p. 81) gives the numbers of households in, and the amounts of total wealth owned by, different income classes, from which a cumulative distribution can be calculated. Log-linear interpolation then produces the estimates of Table 15. One important point regarding these estimates is that, although households with annual incomes over 180,000 DM are excluded from the survey on which the estimates are based, Meirheim and Wicke present figures for both their numbers and their mean wealth. Table 15 is therefore corrected for the omission of these households. The basis for this

TABLE 15

THE DISTRIBUTION OF WEALTH IN WEST GERMANY, 1973

Top ..	1%	5%	10%	20%	30%	40%
Own ..	18·7%	33·9%	45·3%	57·4%	66·1%	73·4%
Top ..	50%	60%	70%	80%	90%	100%
Own ..	79·2%	84·5%	88·8%	92·9%	96·6%	100·0%

Notes:

This Table is based on table 4 in Mierheim and Wicke (1977, p. 81).

correction is discussed by Mierheim and Wicke. They use income tax statistics to derive an estimate of the number of households involved (1977, pp. 62–63); and various sources, such as a study by Euler of wealth composition in 1969, and independent control totals, to allocate wealth to these households.

119   As we mentioned earlier, the figures in Table 15 are likely to be very unreliable because of the many omissions and deficiencies in the asset information on which they are based. Also, the households are ranked by size of income, rather than by size of wealth, and to the extent that correlation between income and wealth is less than perfect, this will tend to understate the percentage shares of top wealth holders. On the other hand, the estimates do not exhibit the very low shares of the bottom 50% usually seen when consumer durables are excluded. The estimated share of the top 1% is higher than the figure for France, which seems strange in view of the fact that the CREP survey in France attempted to oversample the rich. Both surveys however are deficient in a number of respects, so that, once again we are forced to the conclusion that little would be gained by a systematic comparison.

V   IRELAND

120   We come finally to the distribution of wealth in Ireland. The recent figures for this country, estimated by Lyons (1972a, 1974, 1975) and based on estate data, have been the subject of a continuing debate. The original work was followed by a comment on certain aspects of Lyons' use of the estate multiplier method (Harrison and Nolan, 1975), a comment on the comment (Chesher and McMahon, 1976) and finally a reply to the latter comment (Harrison, 1976). Also, controversy has arisen because of the use of Lyons' estimates in political debate without reference to the various well-known problems associated with the estate multiplier method, problems moreover which Lyons readily acknowledges. Notwithstanding this, the estate data in Ireland have allowed construction of estimates which, compared with others based on the same method, are probably matched or surpassed only by those in the UK and the USA. For this reason, as we have already mentioned, we consider Ireland separately rather than grouping it with its neighbours in Western Europe, and at the conclusion of this section we offer some comparisons of the Irish estimates with those for the UK.

121   The base year for Lyons' work is 1966, a year in which a population census was undertaken in Ireland. Because of the small number of estates which are liable for duty in any one year, and their likely unrepresentative nature, Lyons combines the estate duty statistics for the fiscal years 1965–66 and 1966–67, so that, given the normal assumption of a three-month delay between death and payment of first duty, the results represent an "average" for 1965 and 1966.[25] In these years the exemption limit for estate duty in Ireland was £5,000, and below this amount no analysis of estates is published. Above £5,000 the statistics are not available in sufficient detail to allow application of mortality multipliers, so that Lyons was forced to conduct a study of the unpublished data to obtain the information he needed on both "small estates" (under

---

[25]They are not, therefore, estimates for 1966, although this is how Lyons presents them.

£5,000) and "large estates" (over £5,000). The procedures he adopted are discussed at some length in the appendix to Lyons (1972a). In the former case, Lyons had access to daily records of small estates classified by estate size, which were kept until September 1965, but these figures were only relevant to the first six months of the two-year period Lyons was studying, and further-more did not reveal the age or sex of the deceased. The number of estates recorded between April and September 1965 was therefore multiplied by four and taken to be the figure for the two-year period April 1965 to March 1967. To overcome the latter difficulty, "a [ten per cent] random sample of estates with a net value of £5,000 and under in those years was examined" (Lyons, 1974, p. 186) and the results of this survey provided information on the estate size, and the age and sex of deceased, for these estates.[26]

122   To compile the required details of large estates, Lyons adopted a three-stage process. First, the monthly records for the relevant two-year period were examined, and details extracted "of all individuals who paid duty on any portion of their net estates during [this] period" (Lyons, 1972a, p. 180). This posed a number of problems, one of which should be mentioned here. The use of fiscal year data as a representation of the calendar year is based on the assumption of a three-month delay between death and payment of first duty. Lyons however found that in Ireland this delay was often considerably greater, "in many cases amounting to years, and in some to decades" (Lyons, 1974, p. 185) so that the estates referred to some deaths which occurred before April 1965 and were likely to be undervalued. This is always a problem with estate data, as Smith (1974), for example, has found in the USA,[27] and can be overcome by converting older estates to a value consistent with the period under study using price indices. Lyons does not however attempt this, nor does he investigate whether there is any relationship between the length of the delay and the size of the estate.

123   Where some of the information on estates was still lacking, the second stage of Lyons' search involved an examination of other records; if this failed, a "third and last resort" was to investigate the Register of Deaths kept by the Registrar-General. The outcome is a distribution of estates classified by estate size, and age and sex of deceased, and this is actually presented in Lyons (1972a) as Table 6·1. Two other points relevant to these statistics should be noted. First, only estates of those dying aged 20 or over are included in the analysis, so that the resulting estimates of the distribution are for this group also. Secondly, estates or parts of estates located in Ireland but left by individuals domiciled outside Ireland are excluded completely, a standard procedure in the compilation of estate multiplier estimates.

---

[26]The description of the procedures used by Lyons to obtain the necessary information on small estates differs between Lyons (1972a, pp. 183–185) and (1974, pp. 185–186), as do the results of the exercise. Presumably, the earlier technique was later found to be inappro-priate, although no mention of the difference is made by Lyons. In consequence, the estimates of the distribution differ between Lyons (1972a) and (1974). Furthermore, there is also a discrepancy between Table 1 in Lyons (1974, p. 188) and supposedly the same figures in Table 3 of Lyons (1975, p. 344). This is discussed below in paragraph 126.

[27]See above, paragraph 29.

124   The mortality multipliers used by Lyons for his main set of estimates are those derived from the general population mortality rates. Since Lyons assumes that the wealth of each member of the excluded population is zero, the use of these general mortality multipliers should generate higher percentage shares of top wealth-holders than multipliers adjusted for social class (Atkinson and Harrison, 1978a, p. 55). In Lyons (1975), a full study of the effects of different multipliers on the 1965–66 Irish estimates is conducted using a variety of adjustments based on social class mortality data for England and Wales. The estimates of the shares of the top 1 % and 5 % compared with those in Lyons (1974) do indeed fall (Lyons, 1975, p. 346), but the changes are relatively small. However, the appropriateness of using foreign mortality data for the purpose of adjusting multipliers has already been called into question here in our discussion of Gunton's estimates for Australia, and we therefore prefer to confine ourselves to Lyons' estimates using general mortality multipliers, bearing in mind, of course, that the figures for the top wealth-holders will tend to be slightly overstated.

125   Before proceeding to a discussion of these estimates, we should perhaps briefly outline the nature of the exchange, mentioned above, between Harrison and Nolan (1975) and Chesher and McMahon (1976). The main focus of the paper by Harrison and Nolan is the assumption by Lyons that the excluded population has zero wealth.[28] They claim to demonstrate that the assumption is invalid and argue that a figure of £30 per head in 1965–66 would be more appropriate. They recognise however that the effect of this on the estimated percentage shares of top wealth-holders is relatively slight, so that, for example, the top 5 % would own 70 % of total personal wealth instead of 72 %[29]. Chesher and McMahon raise the question of the appropriateness of the test used by Harrison and Nolan in their demonstration of the invalidity of the zero wealth assumption, a criticism which seems to be accepted in a reply by Harrison (1976). Chesher and McMahon also offer a further revision of the estimate of the wealth of the excluded population, the much higher figure of £246 per head.[30] This has a more pronounced effect on the shares of the top wealth-holders: the share of the top 1 %, for example, is nearly 4 percentage points lower than that estimated by Lyons (1975). The critical conclusion which emerges from this interchange is not however the correct estimate of the wealth of the excluded population, but rather that much work still needs to be done on the Irish estimates of the distribution of wealth, concerning itself with, for example, a more thorough investigation of this very question.

---

[28] A second purpose of their paper is to criticise Lyons (1972a), quite rightly, for making an inappropriate comparison between his estimates and Inland Revenue estimates for Britain. Lyons mistakenly uses series A figures for Britain, whereas the closest estimates for a comparison are, of course, those of series B. Lyons (1974) makes the correct comparison however, although Harrison and Nolan fail to acknowledge this.

[29] The figure of 72 % is from Lyons (1972a, p. 169). The corrected figure from Lyons (1974, 1975) is however 63 %.

[30] This is unlikely to be too low, and may be too high. For instance, Atkinson and Harrison suggest a figure for Britain in 1968, two years later than the Irish estimate, of £290 (1978a, p. 109).

126   Log-linear interpolations of the percentage shares from the estimates for Ireland are presented here in Table 16, and two aspects of Lyons' figures should be mentioned before we attempt any comparison of Table 16 with figures for the UK or the USA. First, Lyons notes that the estimate of the total wealth in each wealth range was achieved by multiplying the numbers in each range by the mid-point of that range, taking £700,000 as the mid-point of the final open-ended range (above £400,000).   This is a procedure which he has also adopted in his estimation of the distribution of wealth in Northern Ireland (Lyons, 1972b). Atkinson and Harrison, discussing this work, suggest that "since the data on values of estimates are available for the years of Lyons' investigation, it seems strange that they should be replaced by an assumption, the validity of which is not made clear" (1978b, p. 36). The same comments apply to Lyons' estimates for Ireland presented here. Secondly, there is a small discrepancy between Table 1 in Lyons (1974, p. 188) and Table 3 in Lyons (1975, p. 344), in that the total number of estates in the range £100–£1,000 is given as 301,580 in the former paper and 316,577 in the latter paper. It is clear however from inspection of sub-totals in both tables that the correct figure is that given in Lyons (1975).

TABLE 16

THE DISTRIBUTION OF WEALTH IN IRELAND, 1965–66

Top			1%	5%	10%	20%	30%
Own	..	..	33·7%	63·0%	78·1%	93·2%	97·4%

Notes:

   The Table is calculated from Table 3 in Lyons (1975, p. 344) and refers to the adult population (aged 20 and over). The high figures for groups such as the top 30% reflect the fact that Lyons assumes the excluded population to have zero wealth. The result is that 38% of the total adult population is estimated to own all personal wealth, leaving the remaining 62% with zero. This is equivalent to the assumption on which the series B estimates in Royal Commission (1975, 1976, 1977) are based.

127   The estimated shares given in Table 16 may appear at first sight rather high but much of this reflects the assumption by Lyons that the excluded population has zero wealth. Using the figure of £246 suggested by Chesher and McMahon (1976) as the wealth per head of the excluded population reduces the share of the top 1% to 30%, and that of the top 5% to 57%. Also, the shares in the table are not too different from equivalent (series B) estimates for Britain. The top 1% in Britain owned 33·0% in 1965 and 31·8% in 1966 on this basis, and the share of the top 20% is estimated at 88·8% in 1965 and 87·8% in 1966 (Royal Commission, 1975, p. 102). In the middle 1960s, therefore, at least on the basis of this rather restricted comparison, there was some indication of a broad similarity in the distributions of wealth in Ireland and Britain. If this remained true in the middle 1970s, and if the adjustments carried out on the British estimates were to have a similar effect on Irish figures, the shares of the top 1% and 5% might now be of the order of 25% and 50%, respectively. This is pure supposition however, which is no substitute for the further work which needs to be done on the distribution of wealth in Ireland to provide more precise, more reliable and more recent estimates.

APPENDIX TO CHAPTER 3

128   In Chapter 3 we made reference to certain problems we encountered when we attempted to estimate the distribution of wealth in France from information in Babeau and Strauss-Kahn (1977) and Caisse des Dépôts (1977). This appendix elaborates on these problems and explains how we finally arrived at the figures given in Table 14.

129   We began by attempting to reconstruct the table in Caisse des Dépôts (1977) from Table 20 in Babeau and Strauss-Kahn (1977, p. 132); both are reproduced below as Table A1. The latter has more disaggregated information on the proportions of households in the wealth classes, but, unlike the former, does not list the proportion of total wealth held by the households in each class. Instead, it gives only the mean wealth size for each class, plus the overall mean wealth. The first problem we encountered was that the proportion of households with wealth in excess of 500,000F differs between the two tables. This is probably explained, however, by rounding error, and indeed, the difference, 0·2%, is

TABLE A1(a)

TABLE FROM CAISSE DES DEPOTS (1977)

Wealth range				% of households	% of total wealth
less than 10,000F	..	..	..	31·7%	0·5%
10,000–50,000F	..	..	..	15·7%	2·2%
50,000–100,000F	..	..	..	10·1%	3·9%
100,000–200,000F	..	..	..	13·7%	11·2%
200,000–500,000F	..	..	..	19·6%	33·2%
more than 500,000F	..	..	..	9·2%	49·0%

TABLE A1(b)

TABLE FROM BABEAU AND STRAUSS-KAHN (1977)

Wealth range				% of households	Mean wealth (F)
less than 10,000F	..	..	..	31·7%	2,700(F)
10,000–50,000F	..	..	..	15·7%	26,000(F)
50,000–100,000F	..	..	..	10·1%	73,000(F)
100,000–150,000F	..	..	..	6·4%	126,200(F)
150,000–200,000F	..	..	..	7·3%	174,900(F)
200,000–300,000F	..	..	..	9·4%	249,800(F)
300,000–500,000F	..	..	..	10·2%	377,800(F)
500,000–700,000F	..	..	..	3·5%	583,100(F)
700,000–1,000,000F	..	..	..	2·5%	799,600(F)
1,000,000–2,000,000F	..	..	..	2·7%	1,388,700(F)
more than 2,000,000F	..	..	..	0·7%	2,678,900(F)
Total ..	..	..	..	100·2%	186,800(F)

precisely the amount by which the sum of the items in the column listing the proportions of households in Table A1(b) exceeds 100%. The second problem occurred when we multiplied the figures in this column by the relevant mean wealth and divided the result by the overall mean wealth, expecting to find a more disaggregated version of the final column in Table A1(a). The results are given in Table A2, and indicate that, by so doing, we account for 102·6% of total wealth. This caused us to re-examine the overall mean wealth given by Babeau and Strauss-Kahn. We calculated the weighted mean of the class means, using the proportions of households in the classes as the weights, which yielded a figure of 191,818F. Repeating the exercise described above, and using this latter figure, resulted in the percentages of total wealth given in the final column of Table A2. Log-linear interpolation applied to the cumulated percentages of households and total wealth produced the estimated percentage shares of Table 14.

TABLE A2

ORIGINAL AND REVISED FIGURES DERIVED FROM TABLE A1

Wealth range	% of households	% of total wealth (Mean wealth =186,800F)	% of total wealth (Mean wealth =191,818F)
less than 10,000F	31·7%	0·5%	0·4%
10,000–50,000F	15·7%	2·2%	2·1%
50,000–100,000F	10·1%	3·9%	3·8%
100,000–150,000F	6·4%	4·3%	4·2%
150,000–200 000F	7·3%	6·8%	6·7%
200,000–300,000F	9·4%	12·6%	12·2%
300,000–500,000F	10·2%	20·6%	20·1%
500,000–700,000F	3·5%	10·9%	10·6%
700,000–1,000,000F	2·5%	10·7%	10·4%
1,000,000–2,000,000F	2·7%	20·1%	19·5%
more than 2,000,000F	0·7%	10·0%	9·8%

CHAPTER 4

SUMMARY AND CONCLUSIONS

130   In the preceding three chapters we have discussed the distributions of wealth in Australia, Belgium, Canada, Denmark, France, Ireland, New Zealand, Sweden, the USA and West Germany. We are now in a position to summarise our analysis and to draw some conclusions. We have tended to concentrate primarily on the methods used to estimate the distributions in the various countries, and to pay less attention to the actual results, since the latter are often rather unreliable, and almost always impossible to compare at all precisely between countries. In keeping with this, most of our conclusions relate to aspects of the methods used in other countries which might be usefully applied to the estimation of the distribution of wealth in the UK. We do not offer a "league table" of countries, or any other general comparison of the distributions, for reasons we have outlined more than once earlier. To do so would be to prompt many interpretations for which we would not wish to be responsible.

131   In the countries we have studied can be found examples of all three methods of estimating the distribution, and in one, the USA, use has been made of each of the methods at different times. Mostly, however, all estimates for a particular country have been derived using only one method. France and Canada, for example, use sample survey evidence, while Ireland's estimates are estate-based. The overall picture for all ten countries is summarised in Table 17 which also offers some general remarks on noteworthy aspects of the methods used.

132   In the remainder of this chapter we consider the estimating methods in turn. In each case we discuss the differences in usage between countries, emphasising techniques which are of particular interest in the context of estimation of the distribution of wealth in the UK. We begin with the estate multiplier method.

I   Use of the Estate Multiplier Method in Other Countries

133   Besides those of the UK, we have located estate-based estimates of the distribution in four countries: Australia, Ireland, New Zealand and the USA. A number of other countries have estate taxes, but to our knowledge none uses statistics of the estates covered by the tax to prepare wealth estimates. Of the four countries cited, the USA has the greatest volume of research in this field,[1] and the use made of the estate statistics is appreciably more sophisticated than in any of the other countries. The major disadvantage of the figures for the USA is that they cover only a small proportion of the total population, so that while the shares of the top 1% and 5%, and, with some reservations, the share of the top 10%, can be estimated very reliably, they reveal nothing about the distribution within the bottom 90%. By contrast, the work in Australia, Ireland, and New Zealand using the estate multiplier method

---

[1]The USA is also the only one of the four with official estate-based estimates of the distribution.

TABLE 17

A CLASSIFICATION OF ESTIMATES OF THE DISTRIBUTION OF WEALTH IN TEN COUNTRIES

Country	Method(s) Used	Remarks	Primary Source(s)
Australia	E, S	E-Estate data supplemented by Queensland Succession Duty data. General mortality multipliers adjusted using foreign mortality data/S-Sample survey data appears poor, and probably considerably understate concentration.	E-Gunton (1971) S-Podder and Kakwani (1976)
Belgium	I (+S)	Tax data used, supplemented by sample survey data for assets with zero yield. Details of method (see Walravens and Praet (1978)) are sparse.	Walravens and Praet (1978)
Canada	S	Survey omits consumer durables. Work by Davies (forthcoming) suggests that results understate the shares of the top 5% and 10%.	Podoluk (1974)
Denmark	S	Tax data are the basis of the survey. Details of method are sparse, and use of tax values implies that much wealth is missed by survey.	Sørensen (1978)
France	S	Survey data are poor in spite of attempts to over-sample the rich, often only giving qualitative rather than quantitative impressions of asset holdings.	Babeau and Strauss-Kahn (1977)
Ireland	E	General mortality multipliers used (except Lyons (1975) investigates effects of social class adjustments). Zero wealth allocated to excluded population.	Lyons (1974, 1975)
New Zealand	E	General mortality multipliers used. Zero wealth allocated to excluded population.	Easton (forthcoming)
Sweden	S	Tax data are the basis of the survey. Rich households are over-sampled. Tax values converted to market values.	Spånt (1978)
USA	E, S	E-Much work by, among others, Smith, plus official estimates. Coverage of estate data restricted to small proportion of deaths/S-Sample survey data now rather dated. Work by Ferber et al. (1969a, 1969b) demonstrates problems of non-response.	E-Smith (1974), Natrella (1975). S-Projector and Weiss (1966)
West Germany	S	Sample survey data omit substantial quantities of wealth, including consumer durables. Results probably understate concentration.	Mierheim and Wicke (1977)

Notes: E indicates Estate multiplier method, S indicates Sample survey, I indicates Investment income method.

65

is far more rudimentary in terms of the extent to which adjustments to the basic estimates are made, but the results typically have a greater coverage. For comparative purposes, the estimates for the USA can be used reasonably safely in conjunction with figures for the UK as long as certain qualifications regarding differences in technique and the like are taken account of; those for Ireland, and, arguably, New Zealand, allow of some limited comparison; and the Australian estimates are probably the least reliable in this respect. In what follows, we briefly outline the nature of the estate data used in the four countries, the type(s) of mortality multipliers applied, other adjustments to the basic estimates, and the results obtained.

134 Estate data are made available in varying degrees of disaggregation. In the USA, for example, the principle researcher in the field of the distribution of wealth, Smith (1974) has access to computer tapes containing micro-data on estates. In Ireland, on the other hand, Lyons (1974, 1975) was allowed to sample actual files on estates, painstakingly collecting the data necessary for his study. Both Easton (forthcoming), in New Zealand, and Gunton (1971), in Australia, use grouped estate data, however; and indeed Lyons, as a consequence of his decision to ignore information he had collected on the size of estates, imposes a similar, if not more severe, constraint on his use of the estate multiplier method.

135 In all countries, problems arise with estate data because of different aspects of estate tax legislation. For example, most countries allow some extra exemption for wealth passing to a surviving spouse, so that this is sometimes omitted from estate statistics. Also, valuation of assets at death is not always appropriate for wealth in the hands of the living, an instance of which is life insurance which is valued at sums assured.[2] Unfortunately, reports of research which make use of estate statistics are not always as complete in their description of these problems as one would like. For instance, in the introduction to his work on the distribution in Australia, Gunton remarks that the data he uses "result from calculations by assessors of considerable skill and experience [and] ... cannot be greatly improved on, if at all" (1971, p. 1); he notes that the only "serious" deficiency is that statutory exemptions mean that data are lacking on small estates.

136 At the other extreme is the discussion of the basic data in the USA, in Internal Revenue Service (1976, pp. 61–63). This is a very comprehensive explanation of the differences between wealth assessed for tax purposes and "what is ordinarily considered ... personal wealth", (1976, p. 61), and a number of specific aspects of the estate tax are mentioned. First, in some States all property acquired during marriage is deemed joint property and only half is assessed for tax purposes on the death of one spouse. In the remaining States, joint property is (with some exceptions) taxable in full. Both of these practices are, however, different from that adopted in the UK, in that joint property is not necessarily *all* property acquired by the couple during marriage. Also, at death a special exemption is granted on such property, in addition to the stand-

---

[2]The effect of these on the estimates of the distribution depends, of course, on whether any adjustments have been made to compensate for them, a matter discussed below in paragraphs 140–141.

ard exemption, whereas, in the USA, no such special allowance is exercised. Second, gifts *inter vivos* are taxable only if they are made within three years of death, while before the introduction of capital transfer tax the period during which gifts were taxable in the UK was seven years. The implications of both the special treatment of joint property and the taxation of gifts *inter vivos* for the estimates cannot be established *a priori,* and indeed the latter has been the subject of much discussion in the literature on the estate multiplier method. All that we can be certain about is that some wealth is missing from the statistics because it is joint property; and, depending on who makes gifts to whom, some may be missing also through gifts made more than three years before death.

137 A third difference between estate tax wealth and personal wealth in the USA occurs in the case of assets which die with the individual, for example pensions. This is, of course, a problem common to all countries' estate data, although in the UK, at least, attempts have been made to adjust the final estimates for this omission. The exclusion of these assets from the estimates is usually felt to overstate the shares of top wealth-holders,[3] but as long as marketable wealth is all that we are interested in, the estate valuation of zero is appropriate. This is not, however, true of the fourth difference between estate wealth and personal wealth, the valuation of life insurance policies. In this case the estate valuation of sums assured is clearly inappropriate, and both official and unofficial estimates in the USA make an adjustment to take account of this.

138 As we have mentioned already, the thorough study of these questions in the USA contrasts with the rather optimistic view of Gunton (1971). Both Lyons (1974, 1975) and Easton (forthcoming) appreciate the nature of the problems, although neither makes any adjustment to his estimates. In both Ireland and New Zealand, the treatment of joint property is closer to that adopted in the UK than to that used in the USA; conversely, the period during which gifts *inter vivos* are taxable is only three years in New Zealand as in the USA. All assets which disappear at death remain excluded from the wealth estimates of the two countries, and life insurance policies are valued at sums assured. For this reason, and others, we outline below, in paragraphs 140 and 143–144, the closest UK estimates to those for Ireland and New Zealand for comparative purposes are the series B figures prepared by the Inland Revenue.

139 Turning next to the subject of mortality multipliers, those used in the USA reflect the greater degree of sophistication in the use of the estate multiplier method in this country. In Ireland and New Zealand, Lyons and Easton both use general mortality multipliers, the latter without taking account of differential mortality by sex. Gunton, for the Australian estimates, adjusts the general multipliers by the rather arbitrary procedure of using foreign mortality data where these appear consistent with the mortality experience of the wealthy in Australia. By contrast, in the USA, the official estimates are derived using mortality multipliers adjusted by a very elaborate procedure. Three sets of social class differentials are used, all based on information on insured lives,

---

[3]This is confirmed by the results of both Atkinson and Harrison (1978a, p. 106) and the Royal Commission (1975, p. 89).

and the choice of which set to apply is decided with reference to certain characteristics of each estate tax return. Smith argues however that the resulting multipliers are too high and in the preparation of his estimates uses differentials midway between those for "high status occupations" and those for "affluent individuals" (1974, p. 157). These lower multipliers result in lower estimated shares of top wealth-holders than those in the official figures of Natrella (1975), and are also closer to the social class differentials derived from census data and used in the preparation of estimates for the UK. A further interesting aspect of Smith's multipliers is that they are adjusted to take account of marital status which he has found to be extremely important. Only the most recent Inland Revenue estimates for the UK are adjusted in this respect.

140   None of the sets of estimates for any of the countries under consideration incorporates adjustments to the basic results to the same extent as, say, the Royal Commission in its preparation of estimates for the UK, although, again, this aspect of the estate multiplier method is more highly developed in the USA than elsewhere. For New Zealand, Easton makes the assumption that the excluded population has no wealth and in every other respect his results remain unadjusted. No comparison is made between total estimated wealth and balance sheet totals, no adjustments are made for assets such as life policies, and the effect of assigning the excluded population some positive amount of wealth is not investigated. Gunton and Lyons both attempt to capture some of the wealth which is missed by the estate tax because of the statutory exemptions, although each adopts a slightly different procedure to do this. Gunton makes reference to data from the Queensland Succession Duty which has a lower exemption limit than the Australian estate tax, and assumes that the Queenland estates represent one-seventh of the Australian total. He then extrapolates his estimates to levels of wealth below the Queensland threshold to obtain a figure for all deaths. He does not however ascertain from independent sources whether he has actually accurately estimated the total of all deaths, and in fact his estimate of the total population derived from application of multipliers to his "data" is very much an under-estimate. Lyons' technique, on the other hand is more easily understood. He sampled reported estates below the exemption limit, and assumed that all other estates had zero wealth.

141   Both Natrella and Smith, for the USA, use a total wealth figure from balance sheet data to make estimates of the shares of top wealth-holders. This is equivalent to allocating all wealth missed by estate duty to the excluded population, whereas usually some part is allocated to members of the included population. It is not however so extreme an assumption as it may at first appear since the excluded population represents over 90% of the total population. The other important adjustment which is made to all estimates for the USA is the reduction of insurance policies to equity values. Both Smith and Natrella refer to information supplied by the Institute of Life Insurance on ratios of the cash value to the face value for 11 age groups, and apply these to the amounts of life insurance included in the estate statistics. One further adjustment which Smith alone makes is to examine the dates of all estates and, where necessary, to revalue them to the year of his study. Interestingly, the expected correlation between the length of delay in filing an estate and the size of the estate is not substantiated.

142   This concludes our summary of the use of the estate multiplier method in Australia, Ireland, New Zealand and the USA. Before proceeding to the actual results, however, we first wish to address the question of whether any of the techniques in other countries could usefully be applied in the UK. It must be clear that only the work in the USA has anything to offer in this regard. First, the reduction of life insurance policy values is something which all recent estimates in the USA have incorporated but which has only recently been introduced in the UK, so that the experience of Natrella and Smith will be invaluable. Secondly, a more systematic investigation of alternative mortality multipliers than has previously been conducted in the UK would be very interesting, and the use in the USA of life insurance data for this purpose should provide strong pointers as to how this work might proceed. Until now, only Revell (1967) and Atkinson and Harrison (1978a) have made use of mortality data derived from life insurance records in the UK, and the great deal of research which still remains to be done would benefit greatly from an examination of the procedures described in Internal Revenue Service (1976, pp. 59–60). Finally, Smith's work on mortality differentials by marital status suggests this to be quite important in the preparation of multipliers and, although the most recent Inland Revenue estimates do use multipliers adjusted for marital status, this is still an area which is well worth exploring further.

143   The final aspect of the estate multiplier method we wish to discuss is the outcome of its actual use in each country. From our comments earlier in this chapter and in Chapter 3, it should be clear that we regard the Australian estimates as potentially very unreliable. They suggest that the top 1% and 5% held nearly 29% and 57% of total wealth respectively in 1967–68, if we assume that the excluded population owned zero wealth, but the nature of the adjusted mortality multipliers and the methods used to construct the estate "data" below the exemption limit raise many questions. In New Zealand, according to Easton, the share of the top 1% in 1966 was around 18%. The coverage of the New Zealand figures is higher than that of the Australian figures, accounting for 55·5% of the adult population and the use of the method seems generally more reliable. Easton assumes that the excluded populaton has zero wealth and the closest equivalent UK figures are therefore series B which, in 1966, suggest a share of the top 1% appreciably higher than the New Zealand estimate. One significant drawback of the work of Easton however is the fact that mortality multipliers for both sexes together were used. The effect of this is uncertain and, until it can be clarified, little value can be attached to comparisons between New Zealand and the UK.

144   A more reliable comparison, albeit a somewhat restricted one, can be made between estimates for Ireland and the UK. Lyons assigned zero wealth to the excluded population, and his estimate of the share of the top 1% in 1965–1966 seems at first sight quite high at nearly 34%. In fact, equivalent series B estimates for the UK in 1965 and 1966 are not too different from this, although it is impossible to say whether the trends since that time in the UK have occurred also in Ireland. This brings us, finally, to the estimates for the USA, for which much firmer foundations exist for a comparison with the UK. Tables 3 and 4 in Chapter 2 suggest that the shares of top wealth-holders in the USA at the turn of the 1970s were appreciably lower than those in the UK.

Furthermore, to the extent that the derivation of the estimates differs, adjustments for this will tend to widen the gap, so that overall the share of the top 1 %, for instance, was between two-thirds and three-quarters of the UK figure. On the other hand the share of the top 1 % in the USA hardly changed at all over the twenty years 1953–1972 while, in the first half of that period, the share in the UK fell quite noticeably. The difference in recent years then is much reduced from that observed in the early 1950s.

II USE OF SAMPLE SURVEYS IN OTHER COUNTRIES

145 Sample surveys are probably the major source of data on the distribution of wealth, having been used in recent years in Australia, Canada, Denmark, France, Sweden, the USA and West Germany. At the same time they continue to manifest all manner of problems which lead us to suggest that there currently exists no satisfactory alternative to the estate multiplier method, certainly if estimates of the shares of top wealth-holders are required. Some survey results appear very unreliable, for instance that carried out in Australia, and often the asset data collected are not the primary objective of the survey. In this regard the 1963–64 Survey of Financial Characteristics of Consumers in the USA is very interesting. Its results are naturally now rather dated, but it was in many ways superior to any other survey in terms of the asset data it collected. In spite of this, subsequent work by Ferber et al. (1969a, 1969b) shows that significant response and non-response errors are likely to bias the results, given the survey methods used.

146 In two of the countries considered in this section, Denmark and Sweden, much of the basic information is wealth tax data, which is clearly preferable in some ways to the conventional survey, conducted by interview. Of the two, only the Swedish survey attempts to over-sample the wealthy, a characteristic of a survey which we would argue is essential. Furthermore, the Danish survey is in terms of values established for tax purposes, which for many assets differ from market values. Adjustment to market values is carried out on the Swedish results by Spånt (1978), with the result that the top 1 % is estimated to have held 15–17 % of total personal wealth in 1975. The list of assets covered by the survey is a very comprehensive one, but without more information than Spånt supplies it is difficult to know how much confidence to place in the results. Certainly the use of tax data must offset the standard problems of non-reporting and under-reporting, but the limited scope and coverage of most wealth taxes, including the Swedish one, must still allow much wealth to go unnoticed.

147 Of the remaining countries where estimates of the distribution are survey-based, probably the data with the greatest number of deficiencies are to be found in Australia. These are taken from a survey conducted in 1966–68 in which the "number of families originally approached is not known" (Podder and Kakwani, 1976, p. 78). Hence the response rate is expressed in terms of the number of households successfully interviewed on expenditures. Of these only about 50 % were prepared to supply information on assets, so that there is, to say the least, a strong chance of serious bias in the results. Podder and Kakwani "test" the representativeness of the respondents, but the tests actually offer little, if any, additional information. No over-sampling was carried out, and the

estimated share of the top 1 % of a little over 9 % is so low[4] as to suggest that the survey has really not advanced our knowledge very much. Certainly the comparisons which Podder and Kakwani make with Canadian survey estimates must be heavily qualified given the vastly superior methods used in Canada.

148 In a number of surveys, consumer durables are partly or completely ignored. For example, in the Australian survey, discussed above, only automobiles and other consumer durables bought in the survey years or on which hire purchase payments were still outstanding, were included. In the Canadian surveys they are wholly disregarded. This is regrettable because in other senses these surveys are appreciably superior to many others. In 1970 the sample size was over 23,000 individuals, of whom 67·8 % provided full asset details. Where a refusal was encountered,[5] the missing data were assigned to a non-respondent on the basis of information about him or her which was obtained, such as location of residence, income, sex, age and labour force status. In spite of these efforts, Davies (forthcoming) shows that the survey estimates of the shares of the top 5 % and 10 % are too low. He begins by noting that, while an asset total calculated from the survey typically falls short of one obtained independently, the proportionate extent of the shortfall varies widely. He then investigates the relative contribution of sampling error, differential response and under-reporting to the shortfall and, after suitable corrections, re-estimates the percentage shares of top wealth-holders. Additionally, he makes adjustments for the omission from the survey of consumer durables and insurance equity, and arrives at estimated shares of the top 5 % and 10 % of 45·7 % and 59·8 %, compared with unadjusted estimates of 39·2 % and 53·1 %.

149 Very little information is available on the French survey, conducted in 1975 by CREP (Centre de Recherche Economique sur l'Epargne). Babeau and Strauss-Kahn (1977) do however mention that oversampling of the wealthy was adopted, and that, where significant understatement of assets amounts became apparent from comparisons with independent control totals, some adjustment of an unspecified nature was undertaken. By comparison a detailed description of aspects of the 1973 survey in West Germany is to be found in the paper by Euler (1978). One major problem he cites, the omission from the survey of households with annual incomes in excess of 180,000 DM, is, however, taken account of in the estimates of the distribution of wealth in West Germany in 1973 (Mierheim and Wicke, 1977). Other deficiencies still remain, notably the grouping of households by income size rather than by size of total wealth, which will tend to understate the percentage shares of top wealth-holders. A further problem with the German survey is that some assets are omitted altogether, for instance, consumer durables, and others, such as land and buildings, are valued using out-of-date tax values. The expectation is then that the French results are probably superior to the German results, although a stronger statement than this is not possible in view of the limited information available on the French survey in Babeau and Strauss-Kahn (1977).

---

[4]Gunton's estate-based estimate for Australia of the share of the top 1 % is more than double that of Podder and Kakwani.

[5]"Refusal" here refers only to those households which participated in the survey but which refused to answer asset or debt questions.

150   Finally, we come to the sample survey work in the USA. The results of the SFCC are now of limited value given their age, but the work of Ferber *et al.* (1969a, 1969b) is as relevant today to the whole question of reliability of sample survey estimates as it was at the time it was conducted. They carried out a check on the "reliability of the data collection techniques" (1969b, p. 416) by starting with known holdings of certain assets and then interviewing to see what the holders reported. They found that non-respondents held much larger holdings on average than respondents, so that the mean balance for savings accounts and the average number of shares were understated by 46% and 35% respectively. Their conclusion is a very strong one which casts doubt on the results of even the best constructed surveys: "Improvement of survey procedure can only go so far" (1969b, p. 432). What is required, they feel, is the development of new methods to detect and correct for bias.

151   In the light of our discussion so far in this section, and the fact that there do not exist recent and reliable sample survey estimates of the distribution in the UK, there seems little point in discussing the results of the different sample surveys or comparing them with UK estate-based estimates. In previous chapters, we have only been prepared to make such a comparison on one occasion, and this was between Davies' adjusted Canadian figures and estimates of Atkinson and Harrison (1978a) for the UK. On the basis of this, and when certain differences of procedure are taken account of, the estimated shares of top wealth-holders in Canada fall roughly midway between those for the UK and those for the USA (in 1970). More interesting than the outcome of this comparison, however, is the extent of the revision to the survey shares which Davies (forthcoming) demonstrates is necessary. His work clearly shows the problems associated with the asset data collected in even well organised surveys; we hope that the lesson will be taken to heart if it is decided to launch a major survey in the UK.

III   USE OF THE INVESTMENT INCOME METHOD IN OTHER COUNTRIES

152   This last section is inevitably rather brief since, as Table 17 shows, only Belgium of the countries we have considered makes use of the investment income method. The precise method used, and the results obtained, are discussed in Walravens and Praet (1978), although, as we have mentioned already when referring to other reports of research on the distribution, the details supplied of the method are rather sparse. For all assets yielding a taxable return, the wealth generating that return is estimated using information on appropriate yields, by which means Walravens and Praet account for about 77% of total wealth. They supplement this with data on other assets, for example consumer durables, and life policies, from budget surveys, and claim that their overall results are "close to those obtained" with the estate multiplier method.[6] These results suggest that the top 1% of tax units in Belgium in 1969 held nearly 28% of total personal wealth, and the top 5% nearly 47%. No equivalent estimates exist for the UK, although estate-based figures imply a share of the top 1%

---

[6]Presumably these estate-based estimates are provisional, since we have seen no other reference to them.

which is quite close to the Belgian estimate. Before this comparison can be made more precise, however, much further research is necessary in the UK into the investment income method and the estimates of the distribution of wealth it produces.

REFERENCES

Atkinson, A. B. and A. J. Harrison (1978a), *The Distribution of Personal Wealth in Britain,* Cambridge University Press.

Atkinson, A. B. and A. J. Harrison (1978b), "Wealth", in Maunder, W. F. (ed.), *Review of UK Statistical Sources,* Volume VI, Pergamon Press.

Babeau, A. and D. Strauss-Kahn (1977), *La richesse des Francais,* Presses Universitaires de France.

Barlow, R., Brazer, H. E. and J. N. Morgan (1966), *Economic Behaviour of the Affluent,* The Brookings Institution.

Brittain, J. A. (1978), *Inheritance and the Inequality of Material Wealth,* The Brookings Institution.

Caisse des Dépôts (1977), "Données sur l'épargne des ménages", *Panorama CDC,* May.

Cheng, K., Grant, J. A. G. and H. M. Ploeger (n.d.), *Ontario Estates in 1963–64,* Ontario Committee on Taxation.

Chesher, A. D. and P. C. McMahon (1976), "The Distribution of Personal Wealth in Ireland—the Evidence Re-examined", *Economic and Social Review,* 8, 61–65.

Crothers, C. (1975), "Trends in the Distribution of Private Wealth in New Zealand", unpublished manuscript.

Davies, J. B. (1978), "The Impact of Inheritance on Lifetime Income Inequality in the United States", unpublished manuscript.

Davies, J. B. (forthcoming), "On the Size Distribution of Wealth in Canada", *Review of Income and Wealth.*

Easton, B. H. (forthcoming), *The New Zealand Income Distribution,* NZIER and Allen and Unwin.

Euler, M. (1978), "Methodological and Technical Probems of Recording the Property of Private Households Within the Scope of Household Enquiries", unpublished manuscript presented at the CREP-INSEE international meeting on Wealth Accumulation and Distribution, Paris, July 1978.

Federal Reserve Board (1972), *Flow of Funds Accounts: Financial Assets and Liabilities Outstanding, 1945–71,* Federal Reserve Board.

Ferber, R., Forsythe, J., Guthrie, H. W. and E. S. Maynes (1969a), "Validation of a National Survey of Consumer Financial Characteristics: Savings Accounts", *Review of Economics and Statistics,* 51, 436–444.

Ferber, R., Forsythe, J., Guthrie, H. W. and E. S. Maynes (1969b), "Validation of Consumer Financial Characteristics: Common Stock", *Journal of the American Statistical Association,* 64, 415–432.

Goldsmith, R. W. (1956), *A Study of Saving in the United States,* Volume III, Princeton University Press.

Goldsmith, R. W. and R. E. Lipsey (1963), *Studies in the National Balance Sheet of the United States,* Princeton University Press.

Gunton, R. (1971), "A Distribution of Personal Wealth in Australia, 1967–68", unpublished manuscript.

Harbury, C. D. (1962), "Inheritance and the Distribution of Personal Wealth in Britain", *Economic Journal,* 72, 845–868.

74

Harbury, C. D. and P. C. McMahon (1973), "Inheritance and the Characteristics of Top Wealth Leavers in Britain", *Economic Journal,* 83, 810–833.

Harbury, C. D. and D. M. W. N. Hitchens (1976), "The Inheritances of Top Wealth Leavers: Some Further Evidence", *Economic Journal,* 86, 321–326.

Harbury, C. D. and D. M. W. N. Hitchens (1977), "Women, Wealth and Inheritance", *Economic Journal,* 87, 124–131.

Harrison, M. J. and S. Nolan (1975), "The Distribution of Personal Wealth in Ireland—A Comment", *Economic and Social Review,* 7, 65–78.

Harrison, M. J. (1976), "Comment" on Chesher and McMahon (1976), *Economic and Social Review,* 8, 66–68.

Harriss, C. L. (1949), "Wealth Estimates as Affected by Audit of Estate Tax Returns", *National Tax Journal,* 2, 316–333.

Holmes, G. K. (1893), "The Concentration of Wealth", *Political Science Quarterly,* 8, 589–600.

Inland Revenue (1976), *Inland Revenue Statistics, 1975,* HMSO.

Inland Revenue (1978), *Inland Revenue Statistics, 1977,* HMSO.

Internal Revenue Service (1967), *Statistics of Income–1962, Personal Wealth Estimated from Estate Tax Returns,* US Government Printing Office.

Internal Revenue Service (1973), *Statistics of Income–1969, Personal Wealth Estimated from Estate Tax Returns,* US Government Printing Office.

Internal Revenue Service (1976), *Statistics of Income–1972, Personal Wealth Estimated from Estate Tax Returns,* US Government Printing Office.

King, W. I. (1927), "Wealth Distribution in the Continental United States at the close of 1921", *Journal of the American Statistical Association,* 22, 135–153.

Klebba, A. J. (1970), "Mortality from Selected Causes by Marital Status", in *Vital and Health Statistics,* Series 20, Nos. 8a and 8b, National Centre for Health Statistics.

Knibbs, G. H. (1918), *The Private Wealth of Australia: Its Growth and Distribution,* McCarron, Bird and Co.

Lampman, R. J. (1962), *The Share of Top Wealth-Holders in National Wealth, 1922–1956,* Princeton University Press.

Langley, K. M. (1950), "The Distribution of Capital in Private Hands in 1936–38 and 1946–47, Part I", *Bulletin of the Oxford University Institute of Statistics,* 12, 339–359.

Langley, K. M. (1951), "The Distribution of Capital in Private Hands in 1936–38 and 1946–47, Part II", *Bulletin of the Oxford University Institute of Statistics,* 13, 33–54.

Lebergott, S. (1976), *The American Economy: Income, Wealth and Want,* Princeton University Press.

Lehmann, F. (1937), "The Distribution of Wealth", in Ascoli, M. and F. Lehmann, *Political and Economic Democracy,* Norton.

L'Hardy, P. and A. Turc (1976), Patrimoine des ménages: permanences et transformations", *Economie et Statistique,* No. 76, 3–25.

Louis, A. M. (1968), "America's Centimillionaires", *Fortune,* 77, May, 152–157.

Lundberg, F. (1968), *The Rich and the Super-Rich,* Lyle Stuart Inc.

Lydall, H. F. and J. B. Lansing (1959), "A Comparison of the Distribution of Personal Income and Wealth in the United States and Great Britain", *American Economic Review,* 49, 43–67.

Lyons, P. M. (1972a), "The Distribution of Personal Wealth in Ireland", in Tait, A. A. and J. A. Bristow (eds.), *Ireland—Some Problems of a Developing Economy*, Gill and Macmillan.

Lyons, P. M. (1972b), "The Distribution of Personal Wealth in Northern Ireland", *Economic and Social Review*, 3, 215–225.

Lyons, P. M. (1974), "The Size Distribution of Personal Wealth in the Republic of Ireland", *Review of Income and Wealth*, 20, 181–202.

Lyons, P. M. (1975), "Estate Duty Wealth Estimates and the Mortality Multiplier", *Economic and Social Review*, 6, 337–353.

Mendershausen, H. (1956), "The Pattern of Estate Tax Wealth", in Goldsmith, R. W., *A Study of Saving in the United States*, Volume III, Princeton University Press.

Merwin, C. L. (1939), "American Studies of the Distribution of Wealth and Income by Size", in *Studies in Income and Wealth*, Volume III, NBER.

Mierheim, H. and L. Wicke (1977), "Die Veränderung der personellen Vermögensverteilung in der Bundesrepublik Deutschland zwischen 1969 und 1973", *Finanzarchiv*, 36, 59–92.

Natrella, V. (1975), "Wealth of Top Wealth Holders", paper presented to the 135th Annual Meeting of the American Statistical Association.

Podder, N. and N. C. Kakwani (1976), "Distribution of Wealth in Australia", *Review of Income and Wealth*, 22, 75–92.

Podoluk, J. (1974), "Measurement of the Distribution of Wealth in Canada", *Review of Income and Wealth*, 20, 203–219.

Projector, D. S. and G. S. Weiss (1966), *Survey of Financial Characteristics of Consumers*, Federal Reserve Board.

Revell, J. R. S. (1962), "Assets and Age", *Bulletin of the Oxford University Institute of Economics and Statistics*, 24, 363–378.

Revell, J. R. S. (1967), *The Wealth of the Nation*, Cambridge University Press.

Royal Commission on the Distribution of Income and Wealth (1975), *Initial Report on the Standing Reference*, HMSO.

Royal Commission on the Distribution of Income and Wealth (1976), *Second Report on the Standing Reference*, HMSO.

Royal Commission on the Distribution of Income and Wealth (1977), *Third Report on the Standing Reference*, HMSO.

Sandford, C. T. (1978), "International Trends in the Taxation of Capital", unpublished manuscript presented at the CREP-INSEE international meeting on Wealth Accumulation and Distribution, Paris, July 1978.

Smith, J. D. (1966), *The Income and Wealth of Top Wealth-Holders in the United States, 1958*, unpublished doctoral dissertation submitted to the University of Oklahoma.

Smith, J. D. (1974), "The Concentration of Personal Wealth in America, 1969", *Review of Income and Wealth*, 20, 143–180.

Smith, J. D. and S. D. Franklin (1974), "The Concentration of Personal Wealth, 1922-1969", *American Economic Review*, 64, 162–167.

Soltow, L. (1975), "The Wealth, Income and Social Class of Men in Large Northern Cities of the United States in 1860", in Smith, J. D. (ed.), *The Personal Distribution of Income and Wealth*, NBER.

76

Sørensen, C. (1978), "Study of the Level, Structure and Distribution of Wealth in Denmark", unpublished manuscript.

Spahr, C. B. (1896), *The Present Distribution of Wealth in the United States,* Johnson Reprint Corporation (1970 edition).

Spånt, R. (1978), "The Distribution of Wealth in Some Developed Countries: A Comparative Study of Sweden, Denmark, France, Germany, the UK and the USA", unpublished manuscript presented at the CREP-INSEE international meeting on Wealth Accumulation and Distribution, Paris, July 1978.

Statistics Canada (1957), *Incomes, Liquid Assets and Indebtedness of Non-Farm Families in Canada, 1955,* Queen's Printer.

Statistics Canada (1960), *Incomes, Liquid Assets and Indebtedness of Non-Farm Families in Canada, 1958,* Queen's Printer.

Statistics Canada (1966), *Incomes, Assets and Indebtedness of Non-Farm Families in Canada, 1963,* Queen's Printer.

Statistics Canada (1973), *Incomes, Assets and Indebtedness of Families in Canada, 1969,* Queen's Printer.

Stewart, C. (1939), "Income Capitalisation as a Method of Estimating the Distribution of Wealth by Size Groups", in *Studies in Income and Wealth,* Volume III, NBER.

Straw, K. H. (1956), "Consumers' Net Worth, the 1953 Savings Survey", *Bulletin of the Oxford University Institute of Statistics,* 18, 1–59.

Taussig, M. K. (1976), "Wealth Inequality in the United States", unpublished manuscript.

Terrell, H. S. (1971), "Wealth Accumulation of Black and White Families: The Empirical Evidence", *Journal of Finance,* 26, 363–377.

United Nations (1969), *Demographic Yearbook 1968,* United Nations.

United States Government (1977), *Economic Report of the President,* US Government Printing Office.

Walravens, J. and P. Praet (1978), "La distribution du patrimoine des particuliers en Belgique–1969", unpublished manuscript presented at the CREP-INSEE international meeting on Wealth Accumulation and Distribution, Paris, July 1978.

Wolff, E. (forthcoming), *Estimates of the 1969 Size Distribution of Household Wealth in the US from a Synthetic Data Base,* NBER.

Printed in England for Her Majesty's Stationery Office by Metcalfe Cooper Limited, London
Dd. 586895   K16   4/79